NO B.S. BUSINESS SUCCESS

Dan Kennedy

Self-Counsel Press Inc.
a subsidiary of
International Self-Counsel Press Ltd.

Printed in Canada

First edition: February 1993
Reprinted: May 1993; October 1993; January 1994; June 1995; June 1997
Second edition: February 1998

Cataloging in Publication Data

Kennedy, Dan S., 1954-
    No b.s. business success

    (Self-counsel business series)
    Previous ed. has title: The ultimate no b.s., no holds barred, kick butt, take no prisoners, and make tons of money business success book.
    ISBN 1-55180-143-4

1. Entrepreneurship. 2. Success in business. I. Title. II. Title: The ultimate no b.s., no holds barred, kick butt, take no prisoners, and make tons of money business success book. III. Series.
HF5386.K45 1998   650.1   C98-910064-2

Self-Counsel Press Inc.
a subsidiary of
International Self-Counsel Press Ltd.

1481 Charlotte Road	1704 North State Street
North Vancouver, BC V7J 1H1	Bellingham, WA 98225
Canada	U.S.A.

CONTENTS

PREFACE

*Just a spoonful of sugar
helps the medicine go down.*

R. Sherman, from *Mary Poppins*

Welcome to what I sincerely hope is the most truthful, blunt, straightforward, non-sugarcoated, no pabulum, no holds barred, no nonsense, no B.S. book that has ever been written on succeeding as an entrepreneur.

I have occasionally been introduced as The Professor of Harsh Reality. This does NOT mean I'm negative. If anything, I'm one of the most optimistic, positive-minded people you'll ever meet. However, I do not believe in confusing positive thinking with fantasy. I've discovered that I'm most successful when I have a firm grip on *what is* and least successful when caught wrestling with *what ought to be.*

In this book, I've tried to share, from my 25-plus years of entrepreneurial adventure, *what is.*

If you are already in business for yourself, this book will help you go forward more astutely, efficiently, productively, and confidently. I think you'll also catch yourself nodding as you go along, saying to yourself, This guy has been where I live. Well, sometimes there's value in just finding out you're not alone!

If you have not yet started in business but intend to, this book might scare you off. If it does, consider it a favor; you're too easily spooked to succeed anyway. If it doesn't scare you off, it will help you avoid many pitfalls and problems and cope with those that can't be avoided. It will not cover the basics. There are plenty of very good books out there on the basics — we're not going to cover the same ground all over again. This is not a how-to-start-a-small-business book. This is a go-for-the-jugular success book.

Incidentally, I am not a fuzzy-headed academic, pocket protector and wingtip shoes accountant, or other theorist, although there are plenty of these pretenders writing business books. I'm also not a retired authority who runs a business in my memory. I'm on the firing line every day meeting a payroll, battling the bankers and bureaucrats, struggling to satisfy customers, and solving real business problems. I want you to know this because I think it makes this book more valuable to you.

I'll never forget taking over a company with 43 employees, never having managed more than 2 people in my life. I grabbed every management book I could get my paws on and sucked up all the experts' advice. Then, after a couple of months of getting my brains beat in every day by my employees, I started to look critically at the credentials of those experts. Most of them had never — I repeat, never — managed a workforce. These geniuses spewing out creative management, non-manipulative management, Japanese management, open-door management, and everything-else management wouldn't have survived a week in the real world. I resent those authors to this day. And it's a shame that a lot of college kids get that management theory; that is, fantasy sold to them as reality. So, I chucked all their books, rolled up my sleeves, used my common sense, and started finding out what really works and what doesn't.

Ever since then, I look at every new business book with suspicion. Most won't pass muster because most can't pass the real-experience test.

I also want you to know that there are a lot more things I haven't got a clue about than there are things I understand, and, in this book, I have not dealt with any of the many things

I'm in the dark about. Everything in here is based on my own expensive experience. It may not be right. You may not agree with it. But at least you should know that I didn't swipe it out of somebody else's book, give it a jazzy new psycho-babble name, and pass it off as a new miracle tonic.

I also know you can't eat philosophy. So, while there is a lot of my own philosophy in this book, its primary job is showing you how to make more money than you ever imagined possible, faster than you can believe possible. This is a book about getting rich. If that offends you, please put this book back on the shelf or take it back to the store and get a refund. Spend your money on milk and cookies instead — you'll be happier.

1
THE DECISION AND DETERMINATION TO SUCCEED

*Men are anxious to improve their
circumstances, but are unwilling to
improve themselves. They therefore
remain bound.*

James Allen, *As A Man Thinketh*

Contrary to a great many textbook assertions, having the best product, the better mousetrap, a whiz-bang new idea, the top location, the best market, the smartest accountant, the neatest bookkeeping system, or tons of capital — or all of them together — does not ensure success. On the other hand, having the worst product, a mediocre mousetrap, a silly idea, a bad location, a weak market, an accountant who can't count, a shoe box and paper bag bookkeeping system, or no money — or all of these things together — does not ensure failure.

I have seen people succeed under the most improbable conditions. I've also seen people who have everything going for them still manage to screw it up. In all of these cases, it's the person making the difference. That's why there really are no business successes or failures; there are people successes and people failures.

Entrepreneurial success, like most things in life, is mostly a matter of decision. A partnership, friendship, intimate relationship, or marriage that succeeds or fails, a book that gets written or remains a jumble of notes in a drawer, the garage that gets cleaned out Saturday or put off until next week — these are all the result of decision and then determination to make the decision right. Making the right decisions is often a lot less important than determining to make your decisions right.

Dan Kennedy's Eternal Truth #1
Every successful achievement begins with decision. Most unsuccessful lives are conspicuously absent of decision.

Most people go through life making decisions by default, choosing only from narrow options dictated by others or by evolving circumstances. One millionaire friend of mine grew up in a very small town where, as he put it, there were two career options: working at the factory or raising pigs and chickens. With only a few exceptions, everybody he went to school and graduated with chose one of those two options.

Successful people learn to be much more assertive, proactive, and creative in making decisions. If you are to succeed as an entrepreneur, you have to break free of your old reacting and responding mode and switch to the assertive, proactive mode. You have to reject the entire idea of limited choices.

For most people, the decision to pursue the entrepreneurial lifestyle is the by-product of an evolving dislike for their jobs, frustration with their bosses, or a sudden loss of employment. These days, tens of thousands of people, most middle managers, are being squeezed out of acquired, merged, and down-sized corporations. Accustomed to making $40,000 to $70,000 a year, they are being offered half that — if anything at all — and many are turning to business start-ups as their only reasonable choice.

These people lug a lot of mental and emotional baggage with them. The habits, attitudes, and behaviors that work fine for the employee in the corporate bureaucratic environment, do not necessarily work well at all in the entrepreneurial environment, and must be left behind. The reason why so many new businesses fail is that the owners were unable to leave their old attitudes behind.

WHY TRYING DOESN'T WORK

Some people think and talk in terms of "trying" a business or "trying" out the entrepreneurial experience. Before achieving major success in business myself, I went through considerable agony, corporate and personal bankruptcy, stress, embarrassment, humiliation, and near-starvation. If I'd been just "trying," just taking a test-drive, I'd have quit. And make no mistake about it; my experience is the norm among ultimately successful entrepreneurs.

Rich DeVos plunked down millions to buy the rights to an NBA franchise, The Orlando Magic, apparently to indulge himself. Certainly many envy DeVos as the wealthy, powerful cofounder of Amway Corporation, able to buy a basketball team! But I wonder how many envied him and his partner, Jay Van Andel, when they were barely surviving in business, bottling a liquid cleanser in a decrepit gas station, delivering drums of the gunk cross-country to their few distributors in their own pick-up truck, being laughed at by friends and family.

My occasional client and one of my best friends, Lee Milteer, is universally respected and sometimes envied by her colleagues. Her career as a professional speaker and TV personality is thriving. As a speaker, she routinely commands

3

$5,000 per speech. But when I met Lee, her speaking career was floundering, she was over $35,000 in the hole, pawning jewelry to print brochures, and taking more calls from bill collectors than from clients. In the asset column of her balance sheet, she had little more than a burning desire and determination to succeed in this unusual business.

Although Lee has developed into a very good speaker, I happen to know a number of others, more naturally gifted, more professionally talented, and more skilled than her who failed in their attempts at the business. They "tried" it, couldn't make it work, and went back to work in other jobs. Lee's good-humored determination made all the difference in the world.

MAKING AND KEEPING FAITH
WITH YOUR COMMITMENTS

To succeed as an entrepreneur requires decision and determination — total, unwavering commitment. To keep faith with this commitment, you have to develop and embrace attitudes, habits, and behaviors that are markedly different from most of the people you've known. You have to cut down on time spent with people who are not supportive of your entrepreneurial ambitions. Time spent hanging around fearful people, doubtful people, skeptical people can impair your ability to succeed.

You mean I have to change my friends?

Probably. And the books you read. And the television programs you watch. And a whole lot more. We cannot help being and becoming a product of the ideas we associate with most, of the books and magazines we read, the tapes we listen to, the TV we watch, and the people we spend time with.

As thick-skinned as I believe I am and as much of an independent thinker as I pride myself in being, I admit that my performance and determination vary in relationship to

4

what I'm reading, what I'm listening to, and who I'm hanging around with. Earl Nightingale brilliantly summarized all this: "We become what we think about most." If you are going to become an exceptionally successful entrepreneur, *that* is what you must think about most.

Another way to look at this is in terms of passion. The most successful entrepreneurs I know are passionately involved with entrepreneurship in general and their businesses in particular. They're in love with being entrepreneurs, excited about their products or services, "on fire" with enthusiasm, and that gives them superhuman powers.

You cannot immunize yourself against the influences of the ideas and the people you associate with. There is no vaccination to protect you from negative, anti-business thinking. For that reason, you must immerse yourself in associations that are in harmony with your goals and aspirations.

This doesn't mean that you must socialize only with other entrepreneurs. I have friends who are college professors, corporate executives, actors, athletes, office workers, and so on, but I choose them carefully; they do not have negative attitudes about businesspeople; they do have interesting ambitions within their careers or tied to other, outside interests that are stimulating.

Unfortunately, you are going to discover that the majority of the people, non-entrepreneurs, have a number of set-in-cement biases, beliefs, and frustrations with you, the entrepreneur. Here are some of the big ones you'll run up against.

YOU'RE A WORKAHOLIC

Most entrepreneurs I know experience great conflicts between their commitment to business and other aspects of their lives: marriage, family, civic activities, and so on. Having one failed marriage plus one almost-failed, narrowly rescued marriage in my background, I'm hypersensitive to this conflict, and I'm always working on ways to handle it more effectively.

It's convenient and easy for others to label the determined, passionate entrepreneur as a workaholic — a diseased, neurotic addict guilty of neglecting non-work responsibilities, of not loving his or her spouse or family, of being a self-absorbed ass. It's convenient and easy, but overly simplistic, unfair, and certainly not very helpful.

In reality, the constantly working entrepreneur may be saner and happier than the critics. Most people detest their jobs, yet they continue going to them day after day, month after month, year after year. They spend the lion's share of their lives doing things they find boring and unfulfilling, but lack the guts to do anything about it. They live for the weekend. By contrast, the entrepreneur manages to stay involved in work that is so enjoyable and fulfilling that he or she no longer thinks of it as work.

The lovers, friends, parents, and others who throw around the workaholic label may secretly resent their own "stuckedness" and try to make themselves feel better by attacking you, by making you feel guilty.

We could dismiss the critics as jealous, resentful, and unreasonable just as easily as they label us as workaholics. However, no one wants to go through life married only to a business. We need mates, family, and close friends. And they won't all be involved in our businesses or even in business. We don't get to choose our families and, besides, diversity in social life is healthy and necessary. So, better understanding of ourselves and others, recognition of the special problem we present to others, and creative efforts at preserving balance is all very important.

The problem also, ironically, reveals the greatest of all secrets to entrepreneurial success. One study done some years back by *Venture* magazine and Control Data surveyed and analyzed over 700 entrepreneurs, all of whom had operated their own businesses for at least four years and had annual incomes of at least $90,000. The researchers found that "the lines between work and play are obscured for most successful entrepreneurs." For them, work *is* play.

Dan Kennedy's Eternal Truth #2
If it's work, it won't make you rich.

The typical entrepreneur is constantly initiating new projects, even new businesses, to justify the long work day and to keep the game alive. They are not just motivated by desirable end results; they're equally motivated by the enjoyment and thrill they derive from the whole process of business. They love the "action."

If this is workaholism, I'm guilty. But, also, thanks to near-divorce, aging, long conversations with wiser people, and many other factors, I'm developing an appreciation for balancing that passion with other passions, so that one makes the other even better.

Succeeding in business is a real magic trick. Succeeding in business and having a balanced life is an even greater, more challenging, more worthwhile trick. Since anything and everything is possible for the determined person, why not set your sights on the very best?

Some entrepreneurs manage to involve those close to them in their work-absorbed behavior. Tom Monaghan gratefully tells of his wife's patience when he would always choose a pizza joint to check out whenever they were traveling or on vacation. Some fortunate couples share the same entrepreneurial passion and have that work for them.

But what if you're making the big transition from employee to entrepreneur with a spouse who is happy with your old behavior? Or what if you're in love with someone who cannot survive in a relationship dominated by your entrepreneurial passion?

Some of these relationships end. If yours is to survive, you need to be very aware of the strain that your new entrepreneurial personality, passion, and lifestyle is going to create and take proactive, preventive steps to make up for it. You'll find some ideas in chapter 20 of this book.

YOU'RE A WILD-EYED RISK TAKER, A RIVERBOAT GAMBLER. HAVE YOU LOST YOUR MIND?

One of the things that frightens many people and their loved ones about choosing the entrepreneurial lifestyle is the risk. It's interesting that our society chooses the cautious "be careful" as a means of saying goodbye to a friend. We don't say "be successful" or "be happy," we say, "be careful."

I prefer to be adventurous and "fail forward" all the time. Running a business *is* a risk, but it needn't be foolhardy. I rarely make a decision without considering everything from the best case scenario to the worst case scenario. I try to expect the best and insure against the worst.

Most people see things as black or white: someone is either the meek and mild Clark Kent or the strong and daring Superman. They try to see themselves instantly turning from Kent to Superman and have understandable difficulty conceiving and believing in such a miraculous transition.

Such dramatic overnight makeovers rarely occur. People grow into and with their new roles. You *can* start from where you are and grow to where you want to be. Anxiety about the risks inherent in business is natural. But the real objective of the entrepreneur is to *manage* risk, not to *take* risk.

8

Everybody manages risk every day. For example, statistics indicate that the risk of having a home fire during a lifetime is very high. Some people sensibly manage this risk by installing smoke and heat detectors, checking the batteries periodically, keeping an escape ladder in the hall closet, devising and rehearsing an escape plan with the kids, having surge protectors for major appliances, and so on. This is thorough risk management.

Other people just install a smoke detector and forget about it. They are managing the risk to a lesser degree. Still others do nothing at all. They *take* the risk.

The successful entrepreneur deals only with carefully calculated, measured risk. He or she demands accurate, complete information from associates and advisers and welcomes input and ideas from credible sources. But he or she also knows when to stop and avoids the paralysis of never-ending analysis.

There's a balance between too little and too much caution. Admittedly, the entrepreneur leans more toward risk than the typical employee. In J.R.R. Tolkien's book *The Hobbit*, the wizard Gandalf offers Bilbo Baggins an opportunity to go on a great adventure with the potential of acquiring great riches at the end. Bilbo responds with his perspective on adventures: "Nasty disturbing uncomfortable things! Make you late for dinner."

Somewhere between the extremes of unbridled risk and Bilbo's total aversion to adventure you will find your balance as an entrepreneur. As you gradually develop that sense of balance as a risk manager and decision maker, you'll find that you can function without extreme stress or anxiety.

THE PRICE OF ENTREPRENEURIAL SUCCESS IS JUST TOO MUCH TO PAY

For some, that's true. There are some people who really will be happier and more productive in non-entrepreneurial roles.

But there's also great misunderstanding about the price of success.

Every lifestyle, every choice has its price. The person who follows the old model of staying in a good job with a good company for 40 years pays the price in boredom, frustration, and quiet desperation of unfulfilled, untested potential.

Today, people who try to stay with that model often pay an even higher price: after many years of service, a merger, acquisition, down-sizing, bankruptcy, or even disappearance of an entire industry puts loyal employees out on the street. They must tackle a dynamic, tough job market with outdated skills and face the future without the financial security they believed was guaranteed to them for their loyalty and longevity. Entrusting your success to others in corporate bureaucracies is an increasingly risky business.

THE DECISION OF AUTONOMY

When you depend on others, you collect and store up excuses for failure — like Harry does. Harry doesn't like his too-small, in-disrepair house. He doesn't like his five-year-old, mechanically ailing car. He doesn't like the pile of bills in the kitchen drawer. He hates his job. He doesn't respect his boss. But, wait, the one thing he does have going for him is a book of excuses. He opens it up and sighs with relief: This sorry state of affairs isn't *my* fault. My mother liked my brother more and that gave me an inferiority complex. We grew up on the wrong side of the tracks. My family couldn't afford to send me to college.... And on and on and on.

This is called burying yourself in B.S. If you really want to be a success in business, you need to be *emotionally* independent before you can ever become *financially* independent. I feel fortunate to have discovered a lot about this very early in life.

If I ever got an allowance, it stopped when I was still a little kid. I don't remember it. I do remember earning my spending money very early on. I picked strawberries and packaged tomatoes at the greenhouses behind our community, cleaned stalls at a nearby stable, and washed and waxed cars. I soon figured out that selling was easier than manual labor. I spent my teen years selling.

In my early experiences in direct and multi-level sales, I quickly found out that most of my distributors (even though they were 5 to 25 years older and more "mature" than I was) could not be relied on to have the appropriate literature, samples, and other materials with them at presentations! If I wanted prospects handled properly, I had to take steps to make up for the others' lack of organization, discipline, and reliability; I had to have extra supplies on hand. This business taught me the importance of self-reliance.

The sooner you arrive at accepting 100% responsibility for everything, the more successful you'll be. Go take a look in the mirror. There's the man or woman — the *only* man or woman — who can make you happy, thin, rich, famous, or whatever it is that you aspire to.

The autonomy you develop now will stand you in good stead when your business hits some of the rough roads. One sad truth about business is that you never finish with the same people you start with. Partners, friends, key employees, and others will fall by the wayside for one reason or another as you go along. You will outgrow some. Others will become jealous and resentful of you. I can assure you that, at some point, you will have to make a decision that will be very unpopular with everybody around you. Then you will ultimately have to decide that the only indispensable person in your business is you.

I had to end a 5-year relationship with a business partner who had been my closest, best friend. Not long ago, an 11-year working relationship with a lawyer who had become a friend and who had gone through many battles with me also had to be ended. I've had to fire long-time employees who I like personally. And I've had to put my foot down, have a confrontation, and endure temporary anger and tension in the work environment. But, ultimately, business cannot be run by committee or consensus. You're *it*.

Being *it* is not always fun. But always necessary.

HEY, THAT'S NOT FAIR!

A lot of people respond to their various handicaps, problems, and disappointments with the complaint "It's just not fair." And it sure isn't. For starters, we don't get to pick our parents. There's a flaw in the system right there! Next, most of us aren't movie-star gorgeous. But all this pales in comparison to the biggest injustice and mystery of all — the shocking frequency with which bad things happen to good people.

A young man, Donald R., an honors student, considerate, courteous, and athletically talented, had an accident on the high school trampoline, landed on his back across the frame, and wound up paralyzed in both legs and in both arms for life. He had to make a choice. He could have retreated into isolation, devoted his life to self-pity and bitterness, and lived as a helpless invalid. Instead, Donald R. learned to focus the entire force of his personality through his voice so he could use the telephone, the only tool that lets him travel anywhere in the world while wheelchair bound, to become an enormously successful businessman.

Dialing with a pencil clenched in his teeth, he became one of the most proficient telemarketers in his chosen industry. He supports himself with dignity. He made the money to have a beautiful home custom built with every imaginable convenience and gadget to help him function as if he wasn't handicapped. He became an inspiration to others in his field and to other handicapped people. He is influential in his community, generous to good causes, completely productive, and proud. He enjoys an active social life and a happy marriage.

There's no argument that Donald got dealt a lousy hand. Bad things *do* happen to good people, and sometimes we have little or no control over such things. However, we can control our reactions to the cards we are dealt. After Donald had his accident, he dumped a few cards, drew a few new cards, and changed his hand by choice.

That's why there are always people who pull themselves out of the worst ghettos in America to become successful, prominent businesspeople, top athletes, and good family men and women. Oprah Winfrey is just one example of someone who proves this point. She emerged from the horror of child abuse to become the top female talk show host in America, a talented actress, and a savvy entrepreneur. We choose our reactions. We decide what happens next. Complaining, whining, and proclaiming the unfairness of the situation does nothing to improve it.

I can tell you of any number of times that I've been placed in circumstances that were decidedly unfair. Clients who have reneged on their commitments; associates who took unfair advantage; government rules and regulations that are obviously unjust. I couldn't afford to go to college because my parents couldn't contribute. I also stuttered, severely at one time, and still do occasionally today.

My point is that using these or other inequities as excuses for failure won't make you a success. You may be justified, but you'll still be a failure.

I'm sort of an unjustified success. I'm woefully unqualified for just about everything I do. If you had seen me stuttering and stammering as a kid, you wouldn't have bet a nickel on my future as a professional speaker. As I recall, I got a C in high school speech class and probably deserved worse. The fact that I earn a large income as a writer would be a heart-attack-sized surprise to my English and journalism teachers. I'm responsible for the sale of tens of millions of dollars of merchandise each year through the advertising that

I create, but I have no formal training in that field. Personally, I prefer being an unjustified success rather than a justified failure.

One corner of my office is graced by a huge, stuffed Yogi Bear. He's there to remind me of his favorite saying: "I'm smarter than the average bear." That's me: smarter than the average bear. I'm not necessarily better educated, or better qualified, or better capitalized, or better connected. But "street-smarter." Go ahead, I say, run your best at me. I'll keep figuring out new ways to win faster than anybody else can manufacture new obstacles! *That* is the attitude of the entrepreneur who makes it big.

Some cynic once said, "There is no justice. Only power." As an entrepreneur, you have tremendous opportunity to acquire the power of control over all aspects of your life. I'm not talking about the kind of power you lord over everybody, bullying power, brute power. I mean the power to arrange your life as you desire it to be. To associate with people you really enjoy and benefit from being with, to earn an income truly commensurate with your contributions, to live where you most want to live, to travel or to stay home. Your finances are not controlled by some corporate bureaucracy or the whim of a boss; you write your own paycheck.

I have, for example, arranged my business affairs so that I can take many mini-vacations, linked to business travel, as well as extended vacations without worry. I can work at home and let my office run itself. I never have to sit in rush-hour traffic. I get to pick and choose clients and projects.

You get power by deciding to have power.

2
THE REAL ENTREPRENEURIAL EXPERIENCE: A NO B.S. REPORT FROM THE FRONT LINES

I am only an average man, but, by George, I work harder at it than the average man.

Theodore Roosevelt

THE ENTREPRENEUR AS AN UNPAID GOVERNMENT EMPLOYEE

The entrepreneur suffers more bureaucratic foolishness than you can possibly imagine until you deal with it firsthand. As an entrepreneur, you are drafted into service without compensation as a bookkeeper and tax collector for at least three different governments (federal, state, or provincial, city) and for at least a dozen different taxes, some dealt with twice monthly, some monthly, some quarterly, and some annually. There is nothing that politicians and bureaucrats understand less or that costs and frustrates entrepreneurs more than this enslavement to government.

Some years ago, I had one friend, an owner of a small retail business, who got so angry over all this that one day, when his mail was filled with more letters from government agencies than anything else, he had a heart attack, tax notice clutched in hand.

PRIDE IS SOMETIMES THE ONLY PAY

I think one of the secrets to success is that, no matter what, you have to crawl out from under, set aside, and ignore all the bureaucratic B.S. and the million little irritations and problems in order to keep the process of getting, serving, and satisfying customers as your number-one priority. This is easier said than done. There's so much of the other that entrepreneurs and their typically small, over-worked staffs can too easily fall into the trap of viewing the customer as an interruption and obstacle to getting the necessary work done.

Sometimes, when the problems are overwhelming, pride is the only immediate reward. You'll be hard pressed, for example, to find an entrepreneur who hasn't had the experience of meeting the payroll by the skin of his or her teeth, having nothing left over to take home to the family, having to tell the kids they can't afford this or that, taking calls at home from personal bill collectors, and then lying awake at night, staring at the ceiling, wondering if, at next paycheck time, it will be any different. But pride can keep you going.

Some years ago, my wife worked with me in one business and things got so tough and stayed so tough for so long that she, in my view at the time, cut and ran, and took a job to start bringing home a paycheck. In retrospect, I can tell you that she was afraid, actually terrified, and I stupidly ignored her terror. Her decision was probably the only one she could have made under the circumstances, but at the time I interpreted it as a lack of trust and confidence in me, and I took it hard. I resented it, let it affect our relationship deeply, punished her for it in subtle ways for years, and wound up inflicting deep damage to our relationship — all this to a woman I believe may very well be the best human being I've ever encountered. At the time, I couldn't acknowledge her fears unless I admitted my own, and I didn't know how to do that.

TAKE A TRIP DOWN LONELY STREET

Whether you're winning or losing at the moment, the isolation of the entrepreneurial experience is surprising and dangerous. This was expressed well in an article in *Entrepreneur* magazine (July, 1990) by Beverly Bernstein, who left a job with Mattel Toys to start her own consulting business. After two years, her business was booming and she was earning twice her old salary, but she missed the camaraderie of the corporate workplace. "When you start your own business, you don't have the same collegial relationships as when you work inside a company," Beverly explained. "I missed the laughter and the interchange of ideas. I missed the energy. And I still miss them."

As an employee, many decisions are made for you, many more are arrived at through consensus. A social environment with friendship is provided. And, at the end of the day, if there's work yet undone, in most cases, you go home, shrug it off on the way, and pretty much ignore it. All that changes dramatically when you own the business.

I doubt there's anything as absorbing as the entrepreneurial experience. Pro athletes and their coaches certainly live their businesses, but they have off days, even off seasons, and rest periods. They get paychecks and they don't have to worry about attendance, network viewership, merchandise sales, and budgets. The entrepreneur has to play the game *and* run the business.

It's even difficult to maintain your regular social life. People you used to enjoy getting together with suddenly seem different; their concerns and conversations trivial; their daily experiences so different from yours that there's no longer any common ground. In many cases, their attitudes are so different from yours you can't afford to be around them.

I'M AN OVERNIGHT SUCCESS —
AFTER 20 YEARS

It is only in the last few years that I've experienced substantial, consistently increasing success in my businesses. There were many years of struggle. In the darkest days, I would run around all day telling employees, associates, vendors, and investors not to worry, that I knew what I was doing, that everything would be okay. Then I would lock myself in the bathroom, look in the mirror, and call myself a liar. Not a day went by that I didn't have to convince myself to continue. (Occasionally, such days still occur.)

This tests the very core of your being. I am sure there are tougher tests, such as the real life-and-death tests of character faced by soldiers at war, firefighters, and police officers, or those faced by people diagnosed with terminal diseases. But the tests imposed by the entrepreneurial experience must come in a close second.

Consider, for example, the speaking career part of my business. From 1991 through 1997, I've been one of the featured speakers on tour with famous motivational superstar Zig Ziglar and many "celebrity" speakers on heavily advertised all-day events, addressing tens of thousands of people in each city, in about 20 cities each year, often selling $50,000 to $70,000 or more of my books and cassettes per hour. This has contributed to my being sought out and given other top speaking opportunities, helped raise my speaking fees, and made me the envy of many of my peers. As a result, more than one professional speaker has said to me, "You lucky dog."

I started speaking in 1977. In one year, I gave free talks, selling tickets to my own seminars, in over 100 real estate, insurance, and other sales offices, often to groups of just 3, 5, or 10 people. Sometimes people were inattentive or downright rude; while I spoke, they answered their phones, read their newspapers, and slurped their coffee. It didn't help any that I wasn't a very good speaker.

In my first 10 years of speaking, there were plenty of horror stories. Seminars where hardly anybody showed up and I lost money. Tough, tough audiences. I went on tours of 5 cities in 5 days, driving across the country to make it to each. Countless motel rooms with defective air conditioning, heat, or plumbing. I could go on. *But every business has its own version of such an obstacle course, to brutally separate the weak from the strong.*

EVEN WITH SUCCESS, THERE IS FAILURE

Because the entrepreneur is always innovating, experimenting, and pioneering, there's always failure mixed with success: the new ad, the new product, or the new service that doesn't work — or worse.

A friend of mine, Ted G., sold his company early this year for more than $6 million. He started it 10 years ago with $1,000. The day he strolled into the bank with the $6 million check, he felt that he was a pretty smart, successful, even heroic fellow. A month later, he put together a seminar, promoted it with a major advertising campaign, and lost about $40,000. The three days that he worked, teaching that seminar at a loss, he didn't feel so smart, successful, or heroic.

I know what this is like. In the past, I've gone bankrupt, personally and corporately. I've had my cars repossessed. I've gone from a new Lincoln to a 15-year-old Rent-a-Dent, paid for weekly in cash. I have had so little that had a burglar broken into my apartment, he or she might have left a donation. As a result of the bankruptcies, I was criticized, reviled, and sneered at by professional peers, persecuted by my own trade association, and humiliated beyond belief. To give it all its best spin, let's summarize it as prolonged, profound financial embarrassment.

Today, I say with great gratitude, things are much, much better. But even at the height of success, there's failure. For example, one of the things I do in my direct marketing consulting business is create and produce TV infomercials: half-hour programs that sell merchandise. For every successful show, there are many failures. A client may have put up $100,000 or even more and I may have hundreds of hours invested in a show that tests so miserably its first weekend on the air that there's nothing left to do but dig a large hole in the backyard, shove the master tapes in, say last rites, and walk away. That is not easy to do.

The need to shake it off, regroup, and bounce back, to pick yourself up, dust yourself off, and start all over again, is universal and reoccurring in the entrepreneurial experience.

Dan Kennedy's Eternal Truth #3
Failure is part of the daily
entrepreneurial experience.

BLOOD, GUTS, AND GLORY

The flip side, using my speaking business as an example, is standing there on stage in front of 3,000 people, basking in their laughter and applause, sending them stampeding to the book and tape tables, doing more business in 60 minutes than some stores do in 60 days. In my other businesses, I glory in big orders and unsolicited letters of praise in the mail; planning a new promotion, implementing it, and seeing it work; solving a tough problem; and closing a big sale.

I don't think there's anything like the "high" of entrepreneurial success, of taking the germ of an idea and nurturing it, step by step, embellishing it, developing faith in it, implementing it, making it work, and turning it into tangible, substantial rewards.

It's a kind of glory. Songwriters and musicians talk about the experience of driving down the road, fiddling with the radio, and suddenly hearing their own song come on for the first time. Most pull over to the side of the road and listen in awe to what they've wrought. We entrepreneurs get that same kind of jolt when we see our commercial on TV, our ad in a magazine, our new storefront, our product on the store shelf. Most people never experience anything like this.

And then sometimes you hit it big. Imagine being Bill Rosenberg, a high school drop-out who started a little business in 1946 with $2,500 saved from working two or three jobs at a time seven days a week, twelve hours a day. He has seen his little business grow into the nationwide chain, Dunkin' Doughnuts.

Imagine being Richard DeVos and Jay Van Andel, who started mixing up vats of liquid cleaner, first in their basements, then in a defunct service station garage, and peddling it door to door. Now they can drive up to the giant Amway complex in Ada, Michigan, and contemplate the hundreds of thousands of distributors throughout the United States, Canada, Australia, Germany, England, and Japan.

Imagine being Roy Speer, remembering the inauspicious beginnings of the Home Shopping Channel on a local Florida station with a young woman sitting at a table with a phone and a horn, to give callers the now-famous "toot." What does he feel as he sees his enormous telephone ordering center now?

Behind every entrepreneurial glory story, there's an investment of plenty of blood and guts.

WHAT SEPARATES ENTREPRENEURIAL WINNERS FROM LOSERS?

There's a sign on my office door that reads: "Whatever it takes."

21

That is the entrepreneur's job description: holding your paychecks; loaning money to your business; working long hours; having to sell and motivate constantly; dealing with bankers, lawyers, unresponsive vendors, and other difficult folks. The list could go on. Entrepreneurial management is the solving of a never-ending stream of problems. People who go into business for themselves because they think they will have fewer problems than they had in their previous jobs wear down and wear out quickly.

Carter Henderson, author of the book *Winners*, observed, "To be in business is to be assaulted by relentless adversity and crisis; it comes with the territory." The characteristic that tends to distinguish the winners from the losers is the relentless conversion of problems to opportunities, negatives to positives.

Now, I don't mean that you must incorporate into your life the classic "positive thinking" methodology. I don't believe that whistling in the dark does much to protect you from the bogey-man. If he's in there, whistling won't help. I'm talking about an automatic, action-oriented response that instantly dissects crisis and creates new opportunity. That "entrepreneurial reflex" makes all the difference. Will you be dead-tired or energized at the end of every day? Glum and depressed or good-humored and optimistic? Effective or paralyzed? This "reflex" makes those distinctions.

THE GOOD NEWS

As an entrepreneur, you do get a very special entitlement: you can depend on there being a new door to open whenever another door slams shut. In his book *Think And Grow Rich*, Dr. Napoleon Hill wrote: "In every adversity lies the seed of equal or greater achievement." Just about every really terrific thing that has occurred for me has come out of something really terrible. You may think I'm being a Pollyanna, but if you will dig for it, you will find great opportunity in every adversity.

3
HOW DO YOU KNOW IF YOU HAVE A REALLY GOOD IDEA?

A hunting party was hopelessly lost, deep in the woods. "I thought you were the best guide in all of Canada," complained one of the hunters. "I am," said the guide, "but I think we're in Michigan now."

Wilson Harrell, entrepreneur and business consultant, has a unique way of testing a new product, service, or business idea. He calls it the "Well, I'll be damned!" test. Harrell suggests taking a sample of your idea to at least 20 potential buyers (not friends, relatives, or neighbors!) and see how they react. If they don't say, "Well, I'll be damned" or "Why didn't I think of that?" you do *not* have a winner.

If most of the people do say the magic words, ask them other questions such as, What would you be willing to pay for this? If it were available at that price, would you definitely buy it? Maybe buy it? Why? How would you use it? Do they think it's such a good idea they might want to invest in it? Why? Why not?

23

This brings us to the most important rule of entrepreneurial marketing I can think of.

Dan Kennedy's Eternal Truth #4
You cannot trust your own judgment.
Test, test, test. Then test some more.

Are entrepreneurs impatient by nature? Maybe so, but successful entrepreneurs must learn to be patient sometimes. Testing is one of those times. Anytime you can, anyway you can, test.

ASK YOUR CUSTOMERS

At Stew Leonard's famous store, management regularly meets with groups of customers over coffee and doughnuts to ask them what they like, what they don't like, what they'd like done differently, what they think of a new product or service.

A major electronics and appliance retailer took the trouble of finding out what his stores' customers liked best and least about buying televisions, stereos, and appliances. One comment was so frequent and consistent it stood out like the proverbial sore thumb: people hated having to block a whole day out of their schedules and wait around for the delivery of what they purchased. He developed a system to provide instant delivery with purchase or scheduled delivery, with the delivery time guaranteed within a two-hour range. This service became his main advertising promise — with fantastic results!

ASK YOUR COUNTERPARTS AND COMPETITORS

One of the easiest, quickest research tasks every business owner must do is to go to the library, get the Yellow Pages directories from other major cities, and look through all the advertising in your category of business. You will inevitably find advertisers somewhere doing something nobody in your area is doing, and that should give you some good new ideas. As well, you may also find somebody offering a product or service that you have considered. It won't hurt to call them and talk to them about their experiences. You might even go visit them.

The same holds true for your competitors. You probably can't have a direct talk with them, but you can check up on them. I'm amazed at the businesspeople who never go to their competitors' stores or buy their products. Michelle Comeau, a customer service consultant based in Las Vegas, conducts "incoming call handling audits" for her clients; she'll call all a client's competitors, pretend to be a prospective customer, and ask a lot of questions. From the answers, she can detect areas of opportunity.

DIRECT MAIL

One of my earlier books, *The Ultimate Sales Letter*, is all about how to create good direct-mail campaigns and sales letters, even if you know nothing about writing. I wrote that book because I believe direct mail is the very best way most entrepreneurs have available for marketing their products and services for the simple reason that it is the easiest to test results.

Other types of advertising are much more difficult to test. How do you test a Yellow Pages ad, for example? That same ad is stuck there for 12 months; you can't change it. The most frustrating thing about producing TV infomercials — something I do a lot — is the inability to test different ideas, promises, and offers without actually putting together a show at great expense.

Direct mail offers the unique opportunity to do cheap testing. You can tell a lot from tests as small as a few hundred pieces mailed, depending on the market, lists used, and other factors. This means you can "split-test" one letter against another or one offer, price, or premium against another, for just a few hundred dollars. And, once you find a campaign that works, you can keep on testing other variables cheaply and easily, to try and make it better. Best of all, once you find that success formula, you will probably be able to use it to get consistent, successful results for years.

USE ALREADY-TESTED
DIRECT MARKETING CONCEPTS

But what if you can't test? First of all, you need to know as much as you can about what works and what doesn't in your particular business. You need to do your homework on your industry, your counterparts, your competitors, and your customers. Simply, the more you know, the better your "guess."

Let me tell you a secret. I get paid a great deal of money to "create" brilliant marketing ideas, but I doubt that I've ever honestly done that. Inventing a new idea is a lot of work. Stealing a successful idea is a lot faster, easier, and more likely to yield successful results. So, I try to "steal" whenever I can.

For example, I was recently hired to write a full-page magazine ad for a money-making opportunity, so I needed a "killer" headline. I found the two most successful ads I had seen for other money-making opportunities, took the best parts from each, and combined them into a new headline. Then I changed the details to match my client's offer. This ad is working like gang busters. The headline creation process took me 20 minutes. To have thought it up from scratch could have taken 20 hours.

A friend with a specialty retail store came to me in need of an idea to stimulate a fast surge of cash flow. Fortunately, he had a mailing list of his past customers, so he could get the job done with a great sales letter. I pulled a letter out of my files, one a chiropractor had used to promote a "patient appreciation" event, and said, "Here, sit down and rewrite this letter. Don't change much except the details for your products." It took him only one hour to compose a letter that brought in over $30,000 in 15 days.

Given the right resources, you can go a long way on 100% borrowed, already-proven strategies.

MOVING IDEAS FROM ONE BUSINESS TO ANOTHER

To the best of my knowledge, the drive-up service window belonged to the banking industry before anybody else latched on to it. But it sure does account for a lot of the fast-food industry's sales. It's also used by dry cleaners, video rental stores, and florists. There are probably others using it that I haven't noticed and still others who could and should be using it.

Somebody in the fast-food business "stole" this idea. My vision is of a McDonald's executive sitting in his car in the bank drive-in line on Friday afternoon when it hits him — Hey, I don't think we can fit the milkshakes in the little tube, but outside of that, this could work for us!

Just about every idea came from something already created or used. The very successful "Amazing Discoveries" format for TV infomercials is a cross between a game show and a state fair barker demonstrating the magic slicer-dicer to a gathered crowd. Club Med is a cruise ship set up on land. *Star Wars* is an updated version of the classic Western movie.

HOW TO BE MORE CREATIVE

Most entrepreneurial fortunes are made without brand new ideas. Instead, entrepreneurs tend to alter, combine, and "twist" proven winners. Here are a few of the creativity formulas for getting this done. Look for these or other principles behind everything you encounter. Pretty soon this will be a habit of thinking, and you'll automatically be more creative!

27

(a) *If you can't change the product, change the package.* Cheeseburgers. With bacon, without bacon. Round, square. Now what? After just about everything that could be done to a cheeseburger had been done to a cheeseburger, McDonald's created the McD-L-T. Remember? Keeps the hot side hot, the cold side, cold. The product stayed the same; the package changed.

(b) *Make it bigger.* Big screen TVs, "home theaters." Gilleys, THE largest country-western night club in America. 7-11's Big Gulp.

(c) *Make it smaller.* How about a TV that fits in your pocket? One-serving sizes of pudding, yogurt, microwaveable spaghetti.

(d) *Add to it.* Shampoo plus conditioner in one. Cold capsules enriched with vitamin C. A bookstore-cafe combination.

(e) *Subtract from it.* The convertible (a top-*less* car). Foods with no preservatives. No Appointment Hair Cutters, a successful national no frills chain of salons.

(f) *Do it faster.* The ten-minute oil change. Speed-dialers for telephones. The microwave oven — once thought only saleable to restaurants, by the way.

(g) *Do it slower.* The car wash by hand.

(h) *Do it cheaper.* Cubic zirconia jewelry. K-Mart.

(i) *Do it more expensively.* The Nieman-Marcus Christmas catalog, filled with very pricey, unique gifts, gets millions of dollars of free publicity every year. First-class air travel.

WHAT IF EVERYBODY HATES YOUR IDEA?

A lot of very smart people did nothing but discourage Walt Disney. A lot of very smart people told Dave Thomas the fast food hamburger business was saturated. I'm sure we could fill a whole shelf full of books with similar examples. There's probably a product in every room of the house that was once criticized as a dumb idea.

If you really have faith in your idea, even if no one else does, and you go in with your eyes open knowing you may lose, then — charge! On the other hand, keep in mind that the true entrepreneur marries goals and objectives, not isolated ideas. When one of your ideas does prove itself unprofitable, don't try to raise the dead; move on to the next method of achieving your goals.

In 1941, 8th-grade dropout and bakery delivery man Carl Karcher mortgaged his car for $350 to buy a hot dog stand. His first day's sales were an unexciting $14.75. But, by 1946, more hot dog stands followed, and then hamburgers and "Carl's special sauce" were added. Today, the Carl's Jr. chain includes more than 400 restaurants, all based on serving a top-quality hamburger. The unique factor is what Carl calls "partial hostess service." His are the only fast-food joints where you place your order, sit down with your beverages, and wait for an employee to bring your fresh-cooked food to you, rather than standing around waiting at the counter.

But around 1983, Carl had a bright idea that didn't work out. Like all fast-food places, the bulk of the business was breakfast and lunch. Carl decided to buck that norm and go after the family dinner business. He introduced new char-broiled dinner platters — steak, chicken and fish — at all the restaurants, and invested heavily in advertising and promoting these new items to woo customers in at dinner hour. Even the signs on all the locations were changed from Carl's Jr. Charbroiled Hamburgers to Carl's Jr. Restaurant. Millions of dollars were poured into this new approach.

Instead of adding revenue, the dinner idea confused franchisees, managers, and the public. Average annual sales per location dropped. In 1985, Carl Karcher had to face up to the fact that his Big Idea was a flop. He dug in and started leading his company back to its reliable roots. The signs were changed back, menus simplified, prices cut, and the advertising spotlight returned to the famous charbroiled hamburgers. Sales almost immediately started climbing.

In January 1988, Carl Karcher told *Nation's Business Magazine,* "The stress these last several years has probably been greater than at any time in my life. When you've put in 45 years, you think that everything's going to get easier. Nothing is easy! And I think that's where too many people fail in business — they think they've got it made. It's fun being in business, but there's no risk for the wicked."

Carl Karcher's certainly had many good business ideas during his career, and he has backed those ideas with his faith and with action. But, as his story shows, nobody gets by without having a clinker now and again. You will too. So, go ahead, have the guts to act on those you really believe in — and the good sense to walk away from those that prove unrewarding.

4

POSITIONING YOURSELF AND YOUR BUSINESS FOR SUCCESS

*If you don't think advertising works,
consider the millions of people who now
think yogurt tastes good.*

Bob Orben

Positioning is an advertising buzzword, but it's one of the most important marketing concepts you will ever consider in your entrepreneurial career. One of the definitions of positioning is controlling how your customers and prospective customers think and feel about your business in comparison to other, similar businesses competing for their attention.

I have several specific suggestions about this process. Maybe they'll seem obvious to you, but I can tell you that I have seen many businesspeople overlook the obvious, and cost themselves a lot of money as a result.

POSITIONING STRATEGY #1: WHAT DO YOU DO?

Let's start with the name of your business. The best business name telegraphs what the business does. This may sound elementary, but start looking at the businesses in your town and notice how many of their names, boldly displayed on their signs, do not instantly tell you what the business offers and does. In my home city, there are several very large art and craft supply stores called Michaels. For years, their signage said only Michaels. Recently, I noticed new signs: Michaels' Arts & Crafts. I'll bet they finally discovered something.

Think of the instant print industry. There are three large national U.S. chains named Postal Instant Press, Sir Speedy, and Kwik Kopy. In the case of Sir Speedy, the name is not a marketing advantage and may be a disadvantage. Couldn't Sir Speedy be a dry cleaners? A quick lube shop? A messenger service? Kwik Kopy got the same issue of speed into their name but better described what they do, although many people think of them only as a source of copies, not quality printing. For years, my brother had a shop, General Graphics and Printing, located very close to a Kwik Kopy. He got many customers who had photocopies made at Kwik Kopy but brought their larger printing jobs to him, not realizing that both shops were basically the same. Postal Instant Press would have been a much better name had they located all their shops near post offices.

Of course, all these chains are successful, but you have to ask yourself: could they be more successful with a clearer identity? If you were entering that industry, is there a name that would give you a competitive edge?

Names like Dunkin' Doughnuts, Midas Muffler, Domino's Pizza Delivers, and Minit-Lube are all good examples of names that serve as marketing tools. I think it was a classic case of big corporate stupidity when, after Quaker State bought Minit-Lube, they spent a fortune converting all the locations from red and yellow to green colors, and from the name Minit-Lube to the name Q-Lube. From a name that telegraphs the service to a name that means nothing.

Names can help with positioning. Consider Emergency Chiropractic or Chronic Pain Control Center. Both are names of chiropractic practices. One targets accident victims, the other targets people with long-term, recurring problems. When you develop your business name, product names, and service names, think in terms of telegraphing, of targeting, and of giving yourself a marketing advantage.

Some years back, I was asked to develop a name for a weed-killing product in an aerosol can. I wound up with Kills Weeds Dead. Do you have any doubt about what the product does? Isn't it a lot better than Formula 42X?

POSITIONING STRATEGY #2: PRICE

You'll hear a lot of different opinions about pricing strategy. Personally, I don't think I'd ever want to be in a business that procured its customers with the lure of "lowest prices." You cannot build long-term customer loyalty via the cheapest price. The way you get a customer has great impact on how you will sell to that customer again. There will always be someone willing to offer a cheaper price. If the only thing binding your customers to your company is the lowest price, your business will be as fragile in its tenth year as in its tenth week.

Dan Kennedy's Eternal Truth #5
Live by price, die by price.

In every business I'm involved in, we sell quality, value, service, and unique benefits. We do not sell price.

It's helpful to use the supply-and-demand concept in commanding high prices or fees. In my own speaking and consulting business, the busier I've become, the more selective I've become about accepting clients and projects, and, in recent years, I've been striving to reduce travel. Altogether, this has created a greater demand than supply of me. Because I'm busy and rarely in the office, it may be days, even a week or so before somebody new is able to connect with me. Then I'll check a schedule that may not have room for a meeting for weeks. Even telephone calls have to be scheduled in advance as appointments. For me, this has all proven beneficial. The less available I am, the more I seem to be wanted and appreciated.

So, here's a big, big success secret: find ways to create exclusivity, to portray greater demand than supply.

I also believe that the most stable markets are linked to the highest quality. One of my favorite companies is Omaha Steaks, a thriving mail-order firm. You can buy steaks for less money just about anywhere, but you can't buy better steaks. Their customer service is outstanding, and for that reason customer loyalty is extraordinarily high. The "low end" of that same market has virtually no loyalty, moves from one grocery store to the other, moved by cheap-price coupons in the newspaper. Which type of customer base would you rather have?

POSITIONING STRATEGY #3: IMAGE

As long as I live, I will never forget a bank manager looking me straight in the eye, and in a genuinely sincere, shocked voice saying, "You can't be president of a company — you're not wearing a tie." To be perceived, without risk of exception, as a successful entrepreneur, you must match the image of a successful entrepreneur. To be perceived, without risk of exception, as successful and trustworthy in your field, you must match the image of a successful person in your field.

Places of business, product packaging, literature, and advertising, all are subject to the same image concerns as are individuals' appearances. Whether I walk on stage in a suit or in jeans has nothing to do with the quality or value of the speech I'll deliver, but it will have everything to do with how that speech is received. If I come on in the jeans, I instantly create psychological obstacles to acceptance. I've proven to myself that the most authoritative look makes a difference. At most of my speaking engagements, I sell my books and cassettes. I've tested, with identical types of audiences, tie, sport coat and slacks vs. light-colored suit vs. dark, navy or black, pin-striped suit, and I always enjoy greater sales with the last "look."

Dan Kennedy's Eternal Truth #6
We're taught that you can't judge a book by its cover, but we can't help but judge a book by its cover. You will be judged that way, too.

Is this fair? Of course not. It, unfortunately, allows racist, sexist, and other prejudices to live on. And you can certainly have a lot of moral outrage over it if you want to.

But I'm going to ask you a defining question: Would you rather be right or rich? I call this a defining question for entrepreneurs because it challenges you to be totally realistic and pragmatic, give up your excuses, and succeed. A lot of people would rather live mediocre lives under the protection of the "it's not fair" excuse umbrella than to face the world as it really is and do what is necessary to win. A lot of people will cling to certain beliefs and behaviors even at the expense of desirable results. The most successful entrepreneurs I know are willing to change their beliefs and behaviors whenever that change can facilitate the most desirable results.

Now, don't misunderstand; I'm not suggesting the politicians' chameleon game, changing minute by minute, audience by audience, dressing up for one group, down for the next, telling anybody and everybody what they want to hear with no regard for truth or contradiction, having no core philosophy other than desired results. There has to be a "you" in there somewhere. There has to be a collection of core values not subject to easy change. But there are many things not nearly as important as core values that can be easily modified to permit success.

I once counseled a struggling attorney who couldn't understand why he wasn't attracting or keeping solid business clients. The day he drove me from his office to a lunch meeting in his canary-yellow, four-year-old pick-up truck, I told him why. Of course, he protested mightily; he loved his truck, it was paid for, it shouldn't matter, etc. But his practice started picking up when he started driving a Cadillac.

POSITIONING STRATEGY #4: SELF-APPOINTMENT

When we are kids, our parents "appoint us" old enough to stay home alone, old enough to babysit our younger brothers or sisters, old enough to date, and so on. At work, employers or supervisors "promote us." In all these experiences, there is someone else, some authority figure determining that you are qualified to do a certain thing or handle a certain responsibility. This conditioning is not particularly useful when you step into the entrepreneurial world.

People often ask me: "How do you become a professional speaker?" They're looking for some kind of organized path such as going to a school, passing tests, and, finally, getting appointed as a professional by some kind of group. They're disappointed when I say, "Be one."

Early in my career, I read Robert Ringer's book *Winning Through Intimidation*, which made me understand that the biggest problem with getting to the top is getting through the crowd at the bottom. Ringer suggested simply "leapfrogging" over them. I've done that all my life. But I notice most people waiting around for someone else to recognize them, to give them permission to be successful.

Please understand, *you do not need anybody's permission to be successful.* And, if you wait for "the establishment" in any given field to grant you that permission, you'll wait a long,

long time. And remember, success is never an accident, no matter how it appears to outsiders.

Jay Leno got Johnny Carson's job, arguably the best job in show business. At one time, comedian Gary Shandling was considered the front-runner for that job, and David Letterman was after it, too. But only Leno quietly went out and appointed himself to the job. In his travels, he went to the local NBC affiliates in different cities and towns, befriended the station managers, did promotional spots for them for free, and operated as the self-appointed ambassador of goodwill for the network and the show. By the time Carson retired, Leno was the only candidate with the solid support of all the NBC affiliates. Who told him he could do this? Nobody. He just did it.

Several years ago, I got an invitation to speak at luncheon meetings of the prestigious CEO Clubs, comprised exclusively of corporate presidents in six cities. I'm following in some pretty big footsteps: others who have addressed these clubs include media mogul Ted Turner, Herb Kelleher, CEO of Southwest Airlines, Mo Siegel, founder of Celestial Seasonings Tea, and Wally "Famous Amos."

The invitation really did come out of the blue. Still, it's no accident. The man in charge of these clubs has been on my mailing list for years. All the cumulative publicity I've obtained, the books I've written and had published, other groups I've spoken for, praise from other business leaders, my very active profile in several associations — it's all added up and had an impact and led to this important invitation. I didn't directly ask for this particular speaking opportunity, so, in that sense, you could call this a happy accident. But when you understand how very deliberate positioning made it possible, you'd call it anything but accidental.

A STORY OF POSITIONING SUCCESS

The story of Roger N., who skyrocketed from $5,000 to $50,000 a month in commissions, illustrates how important positioning can be.

Roger had been in the business of selling franchises and business opportunities for nearly ten years, making a very good living, averaging about $5,000 a month in commissions, when he hit on the idea that "selling" was the wrong positioning. By pursuing people, he was chasing them away. He was on the defensive too much.

Roger developed a strategy since copied by many in his industry: early in the process of conversing with and providing information to prospective franchisees, Roger requires them to provide two business or professional references and two personal references. Then, he calls those references and asks them questions, ostensibly to determine the character, integrity, and other general qualifications of the person. He tells these references that he is considering this person as well as several others, for the purpose of granting one of them a very valuable arrangement with his corporation. Well, what do you think happens right after those calls take place?

Right. Those four people immediately call his prospect to tell him they were called and to regurgitate their conversations. The prospect now feels that he is competing and qualifying for the opportunity, not being "sold" the opportunity.

Roger switched his positioning from *selling* to *selecting*. In the first year with his new strategy, Roger's income jumped from $60,000 to over $500,000.

What does this have to do with your shoe store, restaurant, insurance agency, or widget distribution business? Everything! Roger's "trick" shows the income-multiplying power of positioning.

WHO DO YOU THINK YOU ARE?

There's an old story that many speakers have appropriated and told as their own: The featured guest speaker seated at the head table says to the waiter, "Bring me some more butter." The waiter says, "Can't. One pat of butter per person." "Do you know who I am?" asks the frustrated speaker. "Nope," says the waiter. "Who are you?"

"I am a famous author, here tonight as the featured guest speaker. After dinner, I'm going to share my wisdom with all these people. This group has brought me in at great expense. That's who I am. And I want another pat of butter."

"Well," say the waiter, "do you know who I am?"

"No," admits the speaker.

The waiter smiles triumphantly. "I am the man in charge of the butter."

The point of the story is that we all need to maintain some modesty and some appreciation for everybody's right to be important. But in positioning yourself and your business for success, you have to clearly determine who you are, then drive that message home to your marketplace. And it's important to make the right decision. The marketplace will usually accept the positioning you choose for yourself and present to others. You really are in control.

5

HOW ENTREPRENEURS REALLY MAKE MONEY — BIG MONEY!

Humorous writer Robert Benchley admitted that, after 15 years, he had concluded he had no real talent for writing. "But then it was too late," he said. "I can't quit because I'm too famous."

SMALL-BUSINESS OWNER VS. ENTREPRENEUR

Paul Hawken, the extraordinarily insightful expert on the entrepreneurial experience, wrote in his book, *Growing a Business*, "The more exposure I gained to the 'official' world of business, the more I began to doubt that I was in business at all. I seemed to be doing something entirely different. I get that same feeling today when I read most of the standard literature."

When I read that, I said, Me too! And I suspect that many readers of this book may feel that way because I'm writing for the entrepreneur more than I am the small-business owner, and, although they can be the same, they are usually very different.

The typical small-business owner marries a specific, narrowly defined business, manages it, and, essentially, employs himself or herself as a general manager. When you start a business, buy a business, or buy a franchise, you really buy yourself a job, hopefully a very good job. You make money by taking a salary, benefits, and perks. In the long term, you may make a significant sum that you can retire on when you sell your business. If you get rich, it will probably be by stabilizing your first store, then opening a second, then a third, and eventually developing a chain. Your first business may only give you $30,000, $35,000, or $40,000 a year in net income — the equivalent of a good job. Six such businesses, though, may give you $180,000 to $240,000 a year and allow you to become quietly, slowly rich.

There's nothing wrong with this model. In fact, there's a lot that's right about it. There are a lot of millionaires made slowly by very "ordinary" small businesses. According to Thomas Stanley, professor of marketing from Georgia State University and a serious student of the affluent in America, most millionaires make their money "the old-fashioned way: hard work for thirty years, six days a week...in businesses that cater to the needs of ordinary people." His and other research shows that a lot of owners of small businesses get rich slowly and steadily over 30, 40, or even 50 years. This serves to demonstrate that you certainly don't need a revolutionary new mousetrap to get rich; there are still plenty of unexploited opportunities in already-established, proven fields of business, and you can build wealth in any number of these fields just by doing things a hair better than the average.

But true entrepreneurs do things a little different, and looking carefully at how they really make money should open your eyes to new and different opportunities, too.

WHAT ARE YOU GOING TO DO
WHEN YOU GROW UP?

The entrepreneur is *not* married to a specific business. If you ask the typical small-business owner what he or she does, you'll get a narrow, easily understood answer: I own a restaurant. I'm a jeweler. I own a gift shop. The entrepreneur's answer is never that simple. He or she may be 42 years old with parents still trying to figure out what their child is going to do when he or she grows up!

Entrepreneurs, first and foremost, make their money with innovative *ideas*. They are creators much more than they are managers. For this reason, they often start, develop, and sell a business only to move on and do it all over again. Some entrepreneurs who try to stay get forced out by their investors, who correctly recognize that being very talented at creating businesses does not necessarily mean that you are talented in managing a maturing business.

Usually, entrepreneurs are in many businesses, not one, even when it looks like one. This is the case with my clients and friends, Bill Guthy and Greg Renker. Guthy's initial business was an audiocassette duplicating business for speakers and conventions. Then he got interested in using his production capability for proprietary products he could market, not just as a contract manufacturer for others, and that led to a licensing agreement with the Napoleon Hill Foundation for an audio product based on the book, *Think and Grow Rich.* Next, as Bill saw several of the people he was duplicating cassettes for doing well with television infomercials, he decided to produce a TV show to sell *Think And Grow Rich* tapes.

Today, ten years later, the Guthy-Renker Corporation is a $350-million-a-year leader in the infomercial field, and might be defined as an infomercial production company, but under that umbrella is another collection of diverse, ever-changing businesses. For example, behind their "Personal Power" TV program with Tony Robbins is an entire publishing business, cassette-a-month club business, and mailing-list business; behind their Victoria Principal skin-care program is a mail-order cosmetics business.

There's no simple answer to "what do you do?" for Bill and Greg. And, they're in eager search of their next great idea — their next new business within their business. The money made managing the business is mostly made for them by other, hired managers. They make their money with ideas.

THE FORTUNE-BUILDING SECRET OF TOTAL CUSTOMER VALUE

I am amazed at business owners who do not have mailing lists of their customers. I am amazed at the businesses that never do anything when they lose customers. And I am amazed at the businesses that do nothing to maximize their *total customer value* — TCV.

The customer who is satisfied with you and trusts you is an enormous, enormously exploitable asset. Let's say you have a neighborhood dry cleaning business. Most dry cleaners take whatever business comes their way, live on their repeat business, and never think much more about it. But let's think about the entrepreneurial dry cleaner who understands TCV. Here are some of the things you'll see that dry cleaner doing:

- *Aggressively expanding usage of core services by repeat customers.* With in-store displays, bag stuffers, handouts, coupons, and mailings, the entrepreneurial dry cleaner encourages customers to use leather and suede cleaning services, spot removal, fur storage, necktie cleaning, etc. By continually reminding these customers of all the different services offered, the total purchase average per customer, per year *will* increase. If the dry cleaner increases the total purchases of a customer by just $4 per month, or $48 per year, and keeps that customer for 10 years, that's a $480 swing in the plus direction. With just 500 customers, that's $240,000, and if the dry cleaner does that to four outlets, that's a creation of a million dollars!

- *Diversifying into joint ventures or "hosting" other businesses with some logical relationship to his or her own.* The dry cleaner re-arranges the location's layout to free up a corner for a shoe repair shop, and arranges with a local shoe repair shop owner for the repair person to be on premises two afternoons a week. The rest of the time, repair work is dropped off at the cleaners one day, back and ready for the customers the next. Of course, the shoe repair corner also stocks and sells quality lines of shoe polishes, brushes, laces, etc. The dry cleaner and two friends get in the carpet and drapery cleaning business and promote that business to the dry cleaning customers. Several times a year (e.g., Christmas, Father's Day, etc.), the dry cleaner brings in displays of high-quality men's neckties and offers them at very good prices, as "impulse buys" to customers.

- *Exploiting the testimonial and referral potential of the customer list.* Using a criss-cross street directory, the dry cleaner builds a list of all the people who live next door to or across the street from satisfied customers. Then, on a Saturday, using a small army of staff and neighborhood kids, they go out and personally call on these prospects, letting them know that their neighbors are customers, inviting them to try the services, and giving out coupons. Follow-up is accomplished by using a series of postcards sent through the mail. With such a targeted, personalized approach, a large number of new customers are added to the base with nominal expense.

This is the method of maximizing total customer value — and I've used it successfully in my own business. When I go out on a speaking engagement or to conduct a seminar, I'm viewed as a professional speaker, and, in most cases, I'm paid a fee for my services as a speaker. But I'm a very entrepreneurial speaker. When I'm speaking, I'm also acquiring customers with great, long-term potential value. First of all, at almost every speech, I'll offer and sell appropriate, relevant books, cassettes, and home-study courses. Second, those buyers will subsequently get our catalogues, one of our newsletters, and a series of offers by direct mail to create additional purchases. Third, they'll be sold a subscription to one of our newsletters or a tape-a-month program or both. Fourth, they'll be encouraged to attend other, future seminars. Fifth, in many cases, they'll become prospects for our direct marketing conferences, my consulting services, or my direct-response copywriting services. My publishing/mail-order company, Empire Communications Corporation, has many customers who buy from us several times a year, year after year after year, who were acquired by my giving a speech five, eight, even ten years ago.

NETWORKING AND JOINT VENTURES

Today's successful, innovative entrepreneur is very much in tune with the idea of cooperative marketing and with networking with other entrepreneurs for mutual benefit and profit.

In Phoenix, there are hundreds of restaurants. But one restaurant owner also has his own TV cooking show, markets video cassettes, cookbooks, classes, and seminars, arranges murder mystery nights at his restaurant promoted in joint venture with a theater group, runs a catering business, and hosts a "culinary capitals of the world" cruise twice a year.

His cooperative relationship with the travel agency for arranging the cruise is an excellent example of a successful joint venture. The travel agency packages the cruise for him to sell to his customers; they also offer it to their customers *and* promote his restaurant to their customers. In turn, he promotes their travel agency to his customers. They each have nurtured their valuable customer lists. By letting each other tap those customer lists, they both benefit and they both further enhance their TCVs.

Another version of entrepreneurial cooperation is the experience of Alan G., a client of mine. Alan is an expert in buying, improving, managing, and selling all kinds of real estate. He has developed "investor clubs" in five cities, where people interested in this method of making money each pay $1,000 per year in dues, attend a monthly meeting, participate in a week-long "boot camp" with Alan sometime during the year, get a newsletter, and get personal consulting in setting and pursuing their individual investment objectives.

From the dues alone, Alan is able to staff and operate his office, fulfill all the responsibilities to his members, and still net a respectable $125,000 a year. But that's pocket change compared to what he receives for access to these clubs and the members. Sellers of properties, brokers, and partnership managers come to Alan with their very best real estate investment deals and, under certain conditions, he sanctions them to market to his members by appearing at the monthly club meetings. And, of course, he receives a fee for that access.

THE REMARKABLE VALUE OF A DUPLICATIVE MODEL

My client and friend Len Shykind has a collection of a few dozen different business cards framed, hanging on his office wall. All the cards are his own from the various businesses he had struggled with prior to hitting his home run with Gold By The Inch. Len invented the idea of taking gold jewelry chain on spools to high-traffic locations like swap meets and making bracelets to size, on the spot, for customers, rather than displaying and selling pre-sized bracelets. The public loved this concept. Whenever he set up his display, people flocked around — and bought jewelry.

46

Len was smart enough to realize he'd invented a business that just about anybody could do. He had a duplicative model.

Today, there are thousands of Gold By The Inch distributors throughout the United States, Canada, and elsewhere, some full time, most part time, setting up their portable businesses at swap meets, bazaars, in stores, and in kiosks. Together they sell tens of millions of dollars worth of Gold By The Inch every year. In fact, the market was so big and the need for more distributors so great, I produced a TV infomercial for Len to interest people in getting into this business. That program ran on national cable networks for eight years and made Len so wealthy that he was able to take a very early retirement last year.

Tom Monaghan turned a single pizza joint into an empire with a duplicative model for a pizza delivery business. Fred DeLuca created a model for a sub sandwich shop with a unique factor: fresh-baked rolls and a simple operations plan. Today, Subway nips at the heels of the giant with the golden arches!

As you drive down the street and see fast-food franchises, instant printing franchises, and dry cleaning stores, you're seeing the power of duplicative models at work. If you attend a Tupperware party, buy an Amway product, stop in an airport for a TCBY yogurt cone, or have a Dura-clean carpet cleaner come to your home, you're seeing the power of a duplicative model at work. Even without the complexities of creating franchises or distributorships, the duplicative approach makes many entrepreneurs wealthy. My client, Jeff Paul, developed an A-to-Z system for getting clients for financial planners and insurance agents. He packaged it in a home-study course and is now making over $100,000 a month marketing these courses by mail. This approach lets you package your successful experience in a given business and use it to extract a fortune from the rest of your industry.

OUTSIDE THE LINES

If given a shoe store, the small-business owner will manage and promote that shoe store well. But ten years from now, it will still be a shoe store. Give that same shoe store to a true entrepreneur and, ten years from now, you probably won't recognize it!

Maybe, as a child, you were urged to "color inside the lines." This was not great training for entrepreneurial success! As you can see, most entrepreneurs make most of their money "outside the lines."

6
HOW TO CREATE
SALES AND MARKETING
BREAKTHROUGHS

People love to buy.

Bill Gove

Okay, here it is — what you probably bought this book for: a no-holds-barred, no-B.S. revelation about how to get rich, preferably quick.

The big money in the world is made in sales and marketing. Nobody gets rich dusting shelves, changing light bulbs, keeping books, or managing employees. Yet, I'm amazed at how many entrepreneurs let such things suck up all their time, focused on everything and anything but sales and marketing.

So let's get this straight from the start: the place for you to direct your time, energy, creativity, common sense, hard work, and resources is marketing.

Now, the worst marketing mistake you can commit is to be boring. People love to buy when it's a pleasure to buy. The entrepreneur's responsibility is to create breakthrough ideas that foster exciting, positive relationships between the

49

company and its customers. This chapter gives you the very best ways I know to create those kinds of breakthrough ideas.

FIND A MARKET NICHE AND EXPLOIT IT

A market niche is a crack, a crevice, an opportunity gap, sometimes a tiny segment of a market being overlooked, ignored, abused, or very poorly serviced.

I know of a printing company specializing in medical forms for hospitals. They (and their competitors) packaged and sold their various forms in cartons of 1,000, 5,000, and 10,000. Many small hospitals and nursing homes refused to buy from them because they didn't need 1,000 copies of any one form. The president of this printing company took the time to ask how many forms they would buy. He then put out a new catalogue with all their forms priced in packages of 150 for smaller hospitals and institutions and, in short order, they captured the whole market.

The story of Floor Coverings International provides another example. This company recognized that most people can't afford an interior designer when they buy new carpeting for their homes, but that most people also lack confidence in choosing the right color, style, and texture to suit their particular needs. So Floor Coverings International equipped their franchisees with "mobile" stores in vans that go to customers' houses; they provide samples and swatches of different carpets for consideration without the high-priced interior decorator. If they promote this service well, they will have themselves a winner.

FIND A NEW SALES MEDIUM AND
LET IT MAKE YOU RICH

In Arizona, there's an industrial cleaning products manufacturer with a very successful line of citrus-peel-based cleaners and stain removers. For years, they bottled these chemicals in giant drums and sold them to factories, restaurants, hospitals, hotels, and other large institutional buyers. Like every other industrial chemical company, the only sales media they used were industrial sales representatives and catalogues distributed to their customers.

Recently, they made the leap to marketing directly to consumers through a new sales medium — a shopping channel on cable TV. It works for them because their products demonstrate like magic tricks. They're perfect for television. Since their first on-the-air test, they can't bottle the cleaners fast enough. They are "TV bestsellers" and this very different sales media has made these entrepreneurs rich, quick.

The late Bill McGowan, the crusty visionary who put MCI on the map, proved the value of exploring new sales media. He had the daring to market long-distance telephone services via, of all things, multi-level marketing! Through a strategic alliance between MCI and Amway, Amway distributors sold MCI services right along with their own products and subsequently brought hundreds of thousands of new MCI customers on board at a rapid-fire pace. MCI's daring decision to use a controversial, often-criticized sales medium and to form this unusual marriage made millions of dollars.

CREATE A NEW TYPE OF GUARANTEE AND CONFOUND YOUR COMPETITION

I love marketing on the strength of guarantees. For me, nothing's better than finding a way to offer the very best guarantee in a given field.

I've been told that guarantees are outdated, overdone, and no longer effective, but my experience proves this to be nonsense. Good guarantees work just as well today as they did 25 years ago, and they may be more necessary than ever.

Chrysler used this idea not long ago with its 7 Year/70,000 Mile Warranty along with the argument: if you want to know who builds them better, take a look at who guarantees them longer. At the time, this was a ground-breaking guarantee. It left the competition gasping and galloping backwards. It got the public's attention, and it sold a lot of cars. (Eventually, of course, the competition caught up. That's to be expected.)

Years ago, my ad agency had a small chain of eyeglass stores as a client, and we created, I believe before anyone else in the country, the "free eyeglass replacement guarantee." My client ran large newspaper ads featuring this remarkable guarantee — and he brought in a flood of customers. He sucked customers right out of his competitors' stores. His stores kicked butt for nearly a year with this promotion. In one store, sales increased by 800%. Today, big chains, like Pearle Vision Centers, use this same strategy.

Many of the audiocassette courses and business-building systems that I sell from the speaker's platform come with a guarantee, but not the typical 30-, 60-, or 90-day guarantee — I give a full 12-month guarantee. I say, "Use the advice for up to 12 months and, if not thrilled and eager to get more, send back the books and tapes for a full refund." In one instance, with one program, I guarantee that you, the buyer, will make at least $25,000 in 12 months by following its guidance or you can get your money back.

I know of no other professional speaker who offers the kind of strong, clear, straightforward guarantees that I do. In fact, I say that if most people had to guarantee what comes out of their mouths, they'd go mute in a heartbeat. These guarantees give me immense power and my customers great confidence.

DELIVER EXCEPTIONAL CUSTOMER SERVICE AND EARN WORD-OF-MOUTH ADVERTISING

As a customer these days, aren't you frustrated more often than not? I find spending money as tough as making it! Think about all the aggravations you have had as a customer and the number of times you've turned away from a business because of poor service.

I devoutly believe that anyone who consistently and aggressively provides customers with exceptional service will make a fortune.

What is exceptional service? It means different things to different people in different businesses at different times, so I can't define it for you in your business with a general statement. But I can tell you where to look and who to study to get close to it.

Walt Disney preached that customers should be viewed and treated like guests. That's why at Disney World and Disneyland all the employees, from the broom pushers to the managers, learn how to direct people to any attraction and how to answer the most common questions. They are taught that they are important to the success of each guest's visit. The next time you're at a Disney park, stand near a broom pusher for a few minutes. Watch how people go up to him or her and ask questions. Watch how well that employee responds. You'll witness exceptional customer service in action.

My favorite Disney marketing principle is *Do what you do so well that people can't resist telling others about you.* Following this principle gives you marketing leverage. A lot of leverage. If you get one customer from an advertisement, that's one thing, but if you get that customer plus three referrals, who in turn each refer two people, that's nine new customers from leverage rather than from direct monetary investment.

SEEK STRATEGIC MARKETING ALLIANCES

I am about to give you the most powerful secret to extracting outrageous profits from just about any business, so pay attention. There is one marketing guru who charges (and gets) $15,000 per person to teach this single secret to entrepreneurs — and when they have heard him, they cheerfully pay and leave happy.

The secret I reveal is the only known antidote to the biggest, nagging problem of all business, that is, the difficult and very high costs of acquiring new customers.

You may or may not know it, but most businesses lose money on their first sales to new customers. In effect, they "buy" their customers with the hope of profit from subsequent sales. They make an investment in getting their customers, and there is nothing wrong with that.

Certainly, you can build a successful business losing money on every first sale. It's done every day by restaurants, retail stores, and mail-order companies. I do it, too. But I sure don't like it. Anytime I can eliminate that cost out of the business formula, I get very excited. You will too, when you understand that the fastest, most profitable thing you can ever do in business is to "steal" someone else's customers rather than investing your own money in ferreting out customers from scratch.

So how is this done? A few examples will show you.

Thomas G. is an expert in buying foreclosure real estate at enormous discounts, and he wrote a very thorough, very professional, very pricey book about it. He then went to another fellow, who published a newsletter on financial matters, investing, taxes, business opportunities and so on, with 5,000 subscribers. This newsletter publisher had invested a huge amount of money digging up these 5,000 people. He had run ads in magazines, sent direct-mail pieces, and paid for a toll-free number and a staff to take customer calls.

Thomas G. could have taken the same steps to find the same 5,000 people, but instead he struck a deal with the publisher. He provides 5,000 brochures and order forms to be sent out with the next newsletter and offers to split the profits fifty-fifty. Because the publisher likes Thomas G. and his product, and he recognizes that he has a ready market for the product, he agrees. This is the basis for a strategic marketing alliance. One party has the customers; the other party has something "hot" to be sold to those customers. Simple. Sensible.

Thomas G. and his publisher partner sold 800 books. Thomas made $24,000 for minimal cost and he also got 800 new customers for free. He is now in a position to sell other products directly to those people.

Can you apply this to any businesses? Sure you can. Consider the experience of the entrepreneur who opened a little deli and sandwich shop in a less-than-perfect location. He needed to get the word out, so he went to the nearby Exxon gas station, on a very busy corner, in a hot location, and asked them to hand out coupon books to their customers, display a poster advertising the deli, and place plastic sub sandwiches on top of the gas pumps. In return, the deli owner offered the manager and crew one free lunch for every ten coupons returned. As well, he offered to distribute the gas station's own "winterize your car" coupons to his deli customers. Over a three-week period, the deli greeted over 200 new customers.

GET PROFESSIONAL PROWESS ON
A PERCENTAGE

I'm about to suggest hiring an expert or two to help you with your marketing. But, first, a few words about expert advice in general.

There are a lot of "experts" out there very eager to get their hands into your entrepreneurial pockets. Most of them aren't worth the powder it would take to blow them up. Most couldn't run your business or any other for a week. Most couldn't sell their way out of a closet. They may be good song 'n' dance people, but that doesn't mean they can conceptualize a great song, write a musical, or attract crowds to the theater. When you peel away the top layer of veneer, you'll find another layer of veneer.

So, the expert advice I have for you about expert advice is to proceed with great caution. And, I'm an expert!

Never let yourself be intimidated. Ask a lot of questions. Check references. Ultimately, trust your judgment and retain control. And, in the case of getting marketing assistance, get it from people willing, even eager, to be paid based on performance, not on task completion.

You'll be hard-pressed to find a Madison Avenue ad agency that will play this way. If they did, they'd starve. The hard, tough truth is that most of what they do fails to work. It wins awards, it gets talked about, it jazzes up half time at the Super Bowl, but it doesn't sell. That's why most agencies that win the industry's Clio Awards quickly lose the clients for which they created all that award-winning, expensive, but ineffective advertising. That's why in my seminars, when I ask everybody to jot down the brand name of the battery advertised by the famous pink bunny banging his drum, one third to one half of all people write down the wrong brand name.

But every top marketing consultant and every top copywriter I know eagerly looks for clients they can really help, then gets most of their compensation from a small percentage of the sales created and measured. For example, when I develop direct-marketing and direct-mail campaigns for a client, I charge a relatively small fee, but I take 2% to 5% of the resulting sales. My personal objective is to choose projects right and do the work so well that each client winds up paying me $50,000, $100,000, or more over time.

Dan Kennedy's Eternal Truth #7
No one will ever be a bigger expert on your business than you.

Also, keep in mind that the best marketing experts do not tell you what to do. They try to create a partnership with you to combine your unique understanding of your business with their special expertise. Then they do the mechanics.

A good marketing professional can save you a lot of time and trial-and-error experimentation, bring you already-proven ideas from their broader experience, and help you clarify your own thinking.

7
WHY AND HOW TO SELL YOUR WAY THROUGH LIFE

You can succeed if others do not believe in you. But you cannot succeed if you do not believe in yourself.

Dr. Sidney Newton Bremer
Successful Achievement

In this chapter, I'm *not* going to attempt to teach you how to sell — that deserves an entire book and then some — but I am going to make a case for your becoming a master salesperson.

You probably don't like the idea of being a salesperson. If you're like many people, you may think of salespeople as fast talkers — people who talk you into things. You may look at sales as combative: somebody has to lose for the salesperson to win. And you perhaps believe that you can't learn to sell, that there really are such things as "born" salespeople. Finally, like many people, you might think that selling is unimportant in your chosen business.

I am here to tell you that these ideas are all false and must be corrected. If you expect to make any money as an entrepreneur, the mastery of selling is absolutely necessary.

CHANGING YOUR ATTITUDES ABOUT SELLING

Myth #1: Selling is just fast talking.

Selling has more to do with listening than talking. Tests done with telemarketers have demonstrated that those who listened twice as much as they talked wound up booking five times as many appointments. Selling is empathy in action.

Myth #2: Selling sets up a win/lose situation.

Selling can have winners and losers, but it doesn't have to be that way. Personally, my type of selling is win/win; the person buying my ideas, products, or services benefits at least as much as I do. The most successful salespeople uncover, clarify, and fulfill people's strongest needs and desires. My speaking colleague Zig Ziglar's most famous quotation is "You can get anything in life you want by helping enough other people get what they want." Actually, you can get not only anything you want, you can get *everything* you want that way.

Myth #3: Sales ability is hereditary.

Selling is a combination of scientific and technical processes that can be learned by anybody, combined with the human qualities of compassion, empathy, and enthusiasm that exist — or at least potentially exist — in everybody.

Mark McCormack, author of *What They Don't Teach You at Harvard Business School*, looks at it from a different angle. He believes that most people *are* born salespeople, but that we "un-learn" it as we grow up. If you stop to think about it, most kids do have good sales instincts. They're not afraid to ask for what they want — persistently.

I suggest that you, too, were a born salesperson; that you already possess great sales instincts, even if you are suppressing them, and that you have the ability to release those instincts *and* to add new sales skills. With the combination of what you have inside naturally, and what you can learn, you can become a master salesperson.

Myth #4: Selling isn't important to every business.

Many books on business would have you believe that companies fail because of poorly selected locations, ill-prepared management, even bad bookkeeping. I think this is all B.S. *Businesses fail, more often than not, because the owners sit on their butts waiting for something to happen rather than going out and selling.* You can also sell your way out of a lot of the trouble entrepreneurs typically stumble into if you have confidence and competence to sell.

BUT WHEN CAN I STOP SELLING?

I used to look forward to the time that I might be able to take a break from selling. But that's the wrong attitude. As entrepreneurs, we have to be in the selling mode 100% of the time, so we might as well enjoy it.

Entrepreneurs actually need to do more selling than many salespeople. We have to sell and re-sell ourselves on our ideas, goals, plans, and decisions each and every day. We have to sell our associates and our employees on doing the things we want done, the way we want them done, when we want them done. We have to sell our salespeople on our products, our services, our ideas, our leadership, themselves, their futures, on selling. We have to sell our vendors and suppliers that what we want done can be done, can be done by them, should be done by them, can be done when we need it done, should be done when we need it done, and can be done at reasonable costs, under favorable terms. We have to sell our accountants and lawyers on our strategies. We have to sell to our bankers, other lenders, and investors.

The decision is not whether to sell. The decision is whether to do it masterfully and whether to enjoy it.

THE TWO MOST IMPORTANT SALES
YOU'LL EVER MAKE

I believe the most important sale you'll ever make in your life is selling yourself on selling. You must decide to master selling, to enjoy selling, and to sell.

The day you commit to a life of selling can be the day that turns your life around. When you start viewing your activities in the context of making sales, you'll get much more done, much faster, and much more effectively.

The second most important sale is selling you on you. Do you really believe you have what it takes to succeed as an entrepreneur? How you feel about yourself and how you see yourself (self-image) combine to regulate what you permit yourself to do and be, much like the thermostat on the wall regulates temperature. No one can outperform his or her own self-esteem or self-image.

HOW TO BRIDGE THE CONFIDENCE CHASM

For new entrepreneurs, and sometimes for experienced entrepreneurs, there can be a wide gap between the capabilities a person thinks he or she has and the capabilities he or she perceives necessary for the tasks ahead. Facing that chasm can be as intimidating as standing at the edge of the Grand Canyon and contemplating Evel Knieval's motorcycle leap.

It has consistently been my experience that people underestimate themselves and overestimate what's necessary for the success they seek. The millionaire entrepreneurs that I know are not much smarter or more knowledgeable than the average person on the street, nor are they gifted or somehow pre-ordained for exceptional achievement. In many cases, they're not as smart as most people — believe me, I've met some pretty dumb rich people. Just about anybody *could* do what they do, it's just that few *will* do what they do.

One good way to bridge the confidence chasm is to make a point of discovering how little the so-called experts and superstars actually do know. You'll be shocked, as I was shortly after I'd determined that I would build a business as a speaker and seminar leader.

I had given about 30 speeches to sales organizations, clubs, and other groups around Phoenix, and had decided it was time to hang around the real pros at the National Speakers Association to find out how this business was really supposed to be run. By the end of the first afternoon workshop I attended, I was thoroughly depressed — not at how much I yet had to learn but at how little the "superstars" knew! I got over my disappointment when it dawned on me that I was a whole lot farther along than I'd guessed and that I was clearly "qualified" to be a big success in this field.

This is not meant as any kind of criticism of this association. I've had similar experiences with other groups. I've discovered, over and over again, that the chasm between my self-assessment and my perception of the experience of the wizards is easily bridged.

More recent was my entry into the infomercial and video production business. When I went to my first couple of Hollywood videotapings, I was pretty intimidated and I was eager to see the highly paid geniuses at work. To make a long story short, I discovered that the technical know-how was easily purchased, and that the more important sales and marketing know-how could come from me just as easily as anyone else. Shortly after that, I produced my first infomercial from scratch, and I did everything: wrote the script, rented the facility, hired the crew, supervised the taping and edited the show, all for about 15% of the typical Hollywood budget. That show has since made the client quite rich, generating millions of dollars and airing continuously for years.

This is not to say that I haven't made some mistakes in this business. I have — big ones. But I also see the most experienced, supposedly brightest experts in this field making big mistakes now and then, too. Now, based on my actual track record, I'm looked at as one of those top experts.

The bottom line is that success really is simple. There are commonsense fundamentals that make up 80% of the essence of each and every business. These fundamentals are transferable from one field to another. Once you grasp these, it's not difficult to collect or hire the other 20% of specialized knowledge.

You can hire expertise and experience at surprisingly low cost. Some of the smartest people in the world are working for wages, employed by companies founded by "dumb" entrepreneurs. You can also learn what you need to know about the specialized aspects of any given business in a hurry. What *you* bring to the table, and what is not so easily duplicated or obtained, is entrepreneurial guts.

Dan Kennedy's Eternal Truth #9
The ability to win is easily transferred
from one business to another.

Earl Nightingale, one of the most famous success philosophers of all time and founder of the Nightingale-Conant Corporation, once pointed out that if there were no successful examples for you to observe, you could just as easily learn how to succeed from unsuccessful people! All you would need to do would be note what they do, and then do the opposite. That idea applies to every business group I've ever been a part of or consulted in: about 5% of the people in the group rake in 95% of the money. The other 95% of the group represent sustained mediocrity. They have lousy work habits, poor self-images, vague and disorganized goals, waste huge quantities of time, and lack imagination and initiative. By carefully listening to them, you can identify what *not* to think about and talk about; by observing their actions, you can see what *not* to do.

The confidence chasm gets a lot smaller as you realize how basic bridging the gap is.

ANOTHER IMPORTANT SALE

You can't sell what you haven't bought.

I'll often ask businesspeople these questions:

- If you were the customer, would buying from you be the clear, inarguably best choice?

- Why should I do business with you instead of any of your competitors?

- Is your product or service a lot better than anything else out there? How?

It may surprise you to know that most can't answer these questions. They hem and haw, stammer and stutter, and, at best, mutter some goofy slogan.

If you can't answer these questions, you're probably not completely sold on the superiority of what you're selling, and if you're not sold, you can't sell.

In his great book *How I Raised Myself from Failure to Success in Selling,* Frank Bettger revealed that enthusiasm made the difference for him. But I don't believe in acting enthusiastic; I believe in being enthusiastic, and that requires good reasons. You need to structure or re-structure your business, product, service, idea, or promise so that *you* are sold on the superiority of what you offer. After that, convincing others is easy.

To be convincing, you have to be convinced.

8
MAKING MONEY WITHOUT MONEY

The banker asked for a Statement. I said I was optimistic.

Mark Victor Hansen

A little short on cash? Take heart: most entrepreneurial success stories involve one person with little or no money matching ideas, drive, determination, hard work, and other attributes with other people's money. I never let the lack of money (or good credit) hold me back and you don't have to either. If you have a reasonably sound business plan and sufficient commitment to your plan, you can obtain the money you need to make it happen!

In this chapter, I deal with finding the money you need to finance a new business, to reorganize, expand, or diversify your present business, or to buy an existing business. If you happen to have capital and/or good credit, so much the better; I'll show you how to make better use of those advantages. But if you're starting from a "disadvantaged" position, that's okay too.

MONEY ALONE ISN'T THE ANSWER

Money is *not* going to be your problem. But I also want to emphasize that money is not going to be your solution either.

Dan Kennedy's Eternal Truth #10
If you can't make money without money,
you won't make money with money either.

The business battlefield is littered with the skeletons of entrepreneurs who erroneously believed that a big chunk of cash would solve their problems. I've been there. I've believed that, too. I've sold others on that idea. And I've been wrong. I'm sorry to say that I've wasted well over $200,000 in what oil wildcatters call "dry holes," thanks to a stubborn belief in cash as a cure-all. But I've also taken nothing and made it into something.

The most successful entrepreneurs I know, including those who now have tons of money, are like the main character in the once immensely popular, long-running television show "McGyver." McGyver is always getting out of a jam by creating some incredible gadget with whatever happens to be lying around. Entrepreneurs, too, sometimes have to turn thin air, spare parts, and other people's discards into resources with which empires can be built. Drop one of these McGyver-type entrepreneurs out of an airplane into a strange city with nothing else but the clothes on his or her back and $5 cash, and he or she will have an office or store opened and be doing business by the sunrise.

The story of Doug W. exemplifies this kind of unique resourcefulness that successful entrepreneurs need. Doug went broke in a big way in a direct sales business and wound up sitting in his bare house, all the furniture gone, and nothing left but a box of 48 copies of the book, *Think and Grow Rich,* and a dozen broken down auto-dialing (telephone marketing) computers. Doug had used these machines to set up appointments for his salespeople in his now-defunct business. He knew they could work and he believed in them. He had used the books in his classes to motivate his salespeople.

Doug asked himself what resources he could draw on to get some cash. He repaired the auto-dialers so they could be sold as used but operable equipment. Then he got on the phone, calling insurance salespeople, real estate agents, and other salespeople, inviting them to a free seminar on using auto-dialers to increase business. He offered a free copy of *Think and Grow Rich* to anybody who came to the meeting.

Doug called and invited hundreds. About a dozen salespeople showed up. He nervously stood up in front of the group, explained how auto-dialers worked, how he used them successfully, and how others used them. Then he gave a demonstration and offered a unique "rent-and-try-then-buy" offer on the machines he had in stock. That evening, Doug sold eight machines; in the first month he collected $800 from rentals. He discovered that he had a knack for selling this type of equipment.

In short order, Doug found a manufacturer of auto-dialers and convinced him to sell the machines at wholesale as Doug needed them, without an inventory requirement, franchise fee, or other up-front payment. In the next few years, Doug built a large business, with national advertising and sales representatives, selling these machines. He also used some of the profits from that business to invest in a new idea for computer software, and that, too, turned into a very successful business. Doug went from bankruptcy to big money without borrowing a nickel.

The last I talked to Doug, a couple of years ago, he was grooming replacements to run his companies, personally working two weeks a month, and sailing the Caribbean on his yacht the other two weeks of the month.

WHAT ABOUT RAISING MONEY?

I am *not* opposed to raising money. In fact, I believe, in most cases it is necessary to "use other people's money" to get a business from some stage to another. I'm not suggesting that you go through your business life avoiding borrowing or raising capital, but I have seen a lot of people who borrow huge amounts of cash suffer from the erroneous beliefs in the power of that cash. By itself, cash cannot change things for the better.

The bottom line is that there's no point in getting money before, unless, and until you have a solid plan for matching and merging it with other resources for productive purposes.

Now, with that said, let's talk about getting money.

THE MYTH OF THE FRIENDLY NEIGHBORHOOD BANKER

I got my first big business loan from a banker in a small town in southern Ohio. I met him over lunch in a little main street restaurant where "mom" took our orders and cooked our meals. He considered my business plan, but mostly he judged my character. We shook hands on a deal and walked the couple of blocks down Main Street to his bank, where he instructed somebody to get me a cashier's check for $50,000. I signed a simple three-paragraph note, and that was that.

Even then, this banker was a leftover from a bygone age, hidden away in this tiny town. Believe me, it wasn't easy finding him. Unfortunately, your chances of finding a banker like this are even slimmer. Getting face-to-face with somebody who really makes decisions at a bank these days is almost impossible, unless you're a Donald Trump.

However, as bank robber Willie Sutton said when asked why he kept robbing banks, "Banks is where the money's at." So, at some time, to the banks you'll have to go. My experience has taught me three key points about approaching banks for business financing:

(a) Bankers know next to nothing about business.

(b) To work with a banker you have to communicate like a banker.

(c) You need to provide the type of collateral that bankers understand.

These three points need some elaboration.

1. Bankers aren't businesspeople

Bankers generally learn about business through college courses or books, and that means they don't know anything at all about the real business experience. It also means that if you talk to a banker like a businessperson, you'll lose every time!

For example, consider the enthusiasm you, as an entrepreneur, bring with your business idea. In most situations, your enthusiasm is an advantage. Your associates and employees — even your customers — will get caught up in your enthusiasm. So, it would be natural for you to sit there with your banker discussing your progress and your plan with great enthusiasm.

But for the typical banker, your enthusiasm is terrifying. To him or her, who does not and cannot understand and appreciate the reasons behind your enthusiasm, enthusiasm represents wild-eyed optimism.

I ran into this problem with bankers after I had taken control of a very troubled company. Among other problems the company had, almost all its clients owed money and were months late paying. There was also an incredible error rate in the manufacturing and delivery processes, and so customer satisfaction was very poor.

By the end of the first month, I had cut the error level to next to nothing, collected over half the past due monies, and re-established good relationships with many key accounts. I was excited about all this. I knew that we could now move onto the issue of increasing sales and seeking new business. But when I expressed that view to the banker, he reacted with alarm because the accounts receivables total had been reduced. He viewed the sudden jump in collections as a negative, not a positive. He had no idea how bad these account balances were in the first place, so he couldn't understand the importance of getting them cleared up. Second, he could not begin to appreciate the importance of quality control improvements, on which we'd spent so much time and money. He actually asked, "How can you afford to worry about the stuff now? Shouldn't you just be busy getting more business?"

Over six months, the company's monthly sales average dipped by about $10,000, but profits were up. Also, we implemented discounts for cash payments to reduce time spent on credit management, so the ratio of receivables to sales decreased. The net result was positive, but the banker remained alarmed. He kept evaluating only by comparing old numbers to new, and he groused about the lack of receivables and the declining sales. He just couldn't get it. The more enthusiastic I was about our progress, the more he backed away.

2. Communicating with your banker

Somers White is a successful business consultant specializing in helping business owners get bank financing. What is his secret to success? He has no magic, but he does know about bankers. White is an ex-banker himself, and he knows how to translate his clients' situations into information and language the bankers can handle.

Bankers are most concerned with the following:

(a) How much money you need

(b) How your at-risk position compares with theirs

(c) How you can be certain of paying it back

(d) How they can be certain you will pay it back

(e) What will happen if your projections are incorrect

(f) How the bank is protected if everything goes wrong

Most bankers are only minimally interested in what you are going to do with the money. Instead, they will be concerned with your ability to make the payments. If you're borrowing for growth or expansion or reorganization, and you can demonstrate that your current profits and cash flow can handle the added payments, that can get the job done. One or more contracts from stable, credible customers can help.

The least convincing information you can present to bankers are your projections. Bankers view lending based on projections as "gambling." If you're going in the door with projections, understand that you're going to be met with skepticism. You need to do everything possible to add credibility to your projections. It is beneficial to you to have your projections prepared or summarized by a professional accountant and obtain an opinion letter showing that they match actual performance of similar businesses or industry averages. Any other similar evidence, where the thinking has been done for the banker, is helpful.

It may help to think of this process as though the banker were a jury member in a murder trial involving complicated use of exotic poisons. The jurors aren't able to figure out whether the poison could have been administered by basting the corn flakes four days in advance. They have to listen to the testimony of the expert witnesses and make their decision based, essentially, on what those experts tell them is true. You need to trot out your own bunch of expert witnesses.

3. Provide the right type of collateral

Bankers are *not* in the business of making loans; they are in the business of making *safe* loans, and that is why they love collateral.

I think that the fantasy of the typical banker is to see enough totally safe loan opportunities cross his or her desk so that he or she can turn down anything and everything with even a glimmer of risk in it. That's why in some lending institutions with monthly lending quotas or goals, a flurry of loans get approved in the last few days of each month. Early in the month, the banker is holding on to the fantasy, hoping to hit that quota with super-safe loans.

All this means is that you need to provide collateral the banker can understand and that can be easily converted to cash if necessary. It means that the collateral you offer must have its value documented and proven. For example, real estate seems to be a popular type of collateral for most bankers.

THE EASY WAY TO GET MONEY FROM A BANKER

I know of only two methods of getting money from a banker easily: taking over loans that have already gone bad and having special influence.

Bankers are much easier to negotiate with after they have made a mistake, and these days, there are a lot of bankers sitting on bad deals. Many people have started in business or enlarged their existing companies by taking over a troubled, already-financed business. When you use this strategy, you'll inherit delinquent loans and save the bank from defaulting on them. In exactly that position, I assumed about $200,000 in outstanding loans and obtained a new, additional credit line of $50,000 from a bank that otherwise wouldn't have given me a credit card with a $100 limit! And it was done without any discussion of my credit worthiness or collateral.

There's nothing wrong with getting the help of someone who has influence on your banker as long as you keep your business dealings honest and legal. Think about who you know in your network of contacts that might be a good reference for you. In one case, I was unable to acquire a credit card merchant account until the owner of a printing company we were doing a lot of business with interceded on my behalf with his banker.

WHAT TO DO WHEN THE BANKERS SAY NO

1. In the United States

One way to turn a banker's no into a yes is going through the Small Business Administration (SBA), the primary governmental agency involved in financing new businesses.

The SBA most frequently acts as a guarantor, essentially a co-signor, for bank loans in cooperation with participating banks. There are banks as well as accountants and consultants that specialize in dealing with the SBA.

The SBA is also occasionally useful as a source of reorganization or expansion capital. Last year, one client of mine got a $300,000 reorganization and expansion loan from his bank, guaranteed by the SBA, in just three weeks.

You can find out more by asking your banker about that bank's relationship with the SBA, by contacting your local SBA office listed in the telephone directory, or by calling the national toll-free line, 1-800-SBA-U-ASK.

Incidentally, your tax dollars support the SBA, so don't hesitate to try to get a return on that investment. Don't think of the SBA as some type of welfare or only a source of last resort. You have a perfect right to access SBA services.

2. In Canada

In Canada, the Business Development Bank of Canada (BDC) is set up to provide loans, loan guarantees, and other types of financing to help small business. In evaluating a loan application, the BDC considers —

(a) the merits of both the business and the business plan,

(b) the ability to repay, the cash flow, or the projected cash flow, and

(c) the experience of the entrepreneur.

The BDC also offers seminars of interest to small business and CASE (Counseling Assistance for Small Enterprise), which is a nationwide pool of experienced, mostly retired, business people who work on a fee basis to assist small business.

The BDC has offices throughout Canada. You can call to ask questions about available services and literature. You'll find the number in the white pages of your telephone directory.

WHERE TO GO WHEN THE BANKS STILL SAY NO

1.   Credit cards and credit financing companies

Do you know that over one-third of all new small businesses are partially if not wholly financed with credit cards? One of the ten largest commercial airlines in the United States, a national restaurant chain, and a toy manufacturer were all financed, in the beginning, by the owners' credit cards!

If you have good credit, it's not difficult to amass, say, a dozen VISA cards and MasterCards, each with a $2,000 limit — that's $24,000 of available capital. But if you walk into one of those banks and try to borrow $24,000 to start your business, they'll laugh you out the door. Is this logical? Of course not. But it *is* reality.

Of course, there is a danger to this strategy. First, credit card interest is just about as bad as it gets, unless you're borrowing from Murray Kneebreaker down at the pool hall. So, getting money this way is very expensive. Second, filling your credit card maximum freezes your access to any other type of credit. Obviously, you are at unlimited personal risk. But if you understand the risks and the costs and still believe enough in your idea to go forward, I say: go for it!

75

A young couple came to one of my direct marketing seminars $100,000 in debt on their credit cards all from financing their work on a business idea they believed in. With a few corrections in their approach, we got their gross sales from $1,000 a month to $100,000 a month within the year. But that wouldn't have happened if they hadn't had the guts to put themselves behind the eight ball in the first place.

Incidentally, you'll probably find it harder to get new credit cards as a self-employed person. If you are reading this while still somebody else's employee, now is the time to get those extra cards and expand your access to credit. The day you take your employer's name off those applications and insert your own as "self-employed," even though nothing else has changed, even with a spotless credit record, you'll find it tougher.

Another similar source of credit are personal finance companies like Household Finance or Beneficial. These companies do not make business loans, but because most entrepreneurs, at least in the start-up and early stages of business, have to personally guarantee their loans, there is no real difference between borrowing in your name or in the business's name.

I financed my first business with unsecured signature loans and "home improvement loans" secured by household goods, TVs, and an old car. Pretty undignified, but effective.

2. Leasing

Another good commercial source of money is the leasing industry. If you're starting a new business, any equipment you need can be leased, not purchased. In some cases, even used equipment and furniture can be leased, which usually means a lower down payment. That means less money sunk into fixed assets, leaving you with more operating capital.

Commercial leasing companies are often "looser" than other lenders. One reason for this is their familiarity with the equipment they're leasing. Remember, bankers don't understand business equipment, have no market for it if they have to repossess it, and, as a result, figure it at a very low value in the worst case scenario. The lessor, though, understands the equipment, does have a market for it, and will give it a higher value in the worst case scenario.

When it comes time to find money for expansion, diversification, problem-solving or some other purpose, the leasing industry may again prove helpful, this time with a sale/leaseback. In just about every industry, there are at least several leasing companies that specialize in sale/leaseback transactions on used equipment. You can "package" your paid-for or even partially-paid-for specialized equipment as well as furniture, fixtures, and similar assets, sell it all to the leasing company for cash, and lease it back. You can pull cash out and, sometimes, gain a tax advantage in the new lease.

Keep this in mind if you buy an established business too. Ben and Susan C. bought a copy shop as a means of expanding their directory publishing business. The deal required a $15,000 down payment — every penny of reserve capital they had plus some money borrowed from friends and relatives. But within just ten days of buying the business, they pulled $17,000 out of a sale/leaseback on all the shop's equipment.

3. Insurance companies

Most insurance companies have both venture capital and business lending operations, usually dealing with very large deals. If you're playing in the $500,000 and up range, you may want to investigate this. The place to start is with the main offices of each major insurance corporation. You can also find more information about this type of financing in any number of books devoted exclusively to the subject of venture capital, which can be found at your main public library. Your banker or accountant should be able to provide some information about this, too.

If your needs are less, you might consider your personal insurance portfolio. If you happen to have whole life or universal life policies, you may have accumulated cash value that can be taken out or borrowed against. You can replace the true insurance coverage with term insurance for much lower premiums. If you're looking for ways to reduce your personal expenses while starting or expanding your business, take a look at the deductibles in your home, car, and health insurance. By increasing these deductibles, you may be able to drop your premiums by a thousand dollars or more a year.

4. Your vendors

Vendors who are eager to make sales and acquire customers will do the most amazing things. Suppliers can be persuaded to use liberal, extended, creative credit terms as a means of obtaining new business. Or, if you've been in business for some time and have good relationships with key vendors, you can get them to alter terms to your advantage. You can even play one vendor against the other. Getting vendors involved as financing sources is a smart, effective strategy in all sorts of circumstances.

Dan Kennedy's Eternal Truth #11
There is no such thing as "standard terms."

Sometimes vendors can even be induced to make outright investments or loans into a business they supply, with the immediate benefit of "locking in" the business plus the future possibility of acquiring the business. This kind of vertical investment, acquisition, and expansion is quite common. For example, Pepsi owns Pizza Hut and Taco Bell, and Quaker State Oil bought Minit-Lube.

WHERE DOES MOST ENTREPRENEURIAL MONEY REALLY COME FROM?

You can add all these commercial sources together and not equal the contribution to entrepreneurial capital made by private sources. Arthur Lipper, former publisher of *Venture* magazine, concluded that the majority of new business capital is "pillow capital"; obtained from spouses or close family members. This has not been my personal experience, but I still agree with Lipper overall.

1. Family

Of course, there are some obvious disadvantages to obtaining business financing from your family. Blood is *not* thicker than water when one relative is late making promised payments to another. But there are two big advantages to tapping this source: first, your family members are readily accessible, and second, they often feel somewhat obligated to be helpful.

If you are reluctant to go this route, I'd question the sincerity and strength of your commitment to your plan. If you believe that nobody in your family has money to lend, you're making a mistake. Believe me, you can't even be sure what your husband or wife has squirreled away, let alone what parents, uncles and aunts, etc. have or have access to. The only way to know for sure is to ask.

One of the most successful entrepreneurs I know started over in business after a bankruptcy with money borrowed from his three kids' college savings accounts and by getting his brother-in-law to take a $1,000 cash advance on his MasterCard. Today, he's got a multi-million dollar a year business that employs all three kids and the brother-in-law.

2. Friends

It's been my experience that the best place to go for start-up money is your own circle of friends and coworkers. These people are accessible, but not quite as close as family, so they may have a more balanced view of your faults and your talents.

Here, too, it's important to never prejudge. I remember casually talking to some friends one day about my business's need for a cash infusion, and a friend's kid brother cornered me and said that he thought he could provide the $10,000. Where, I asked, would he, a 18-year-old kid, get that kind of money? Well, as unbelievable as it sounds, he had it in nickels, dimes, and quarters in coffee cans under his bed! He worked Friday and Saturday nights at an ultra-expensive restaurant parking cars, and he only banked or spent the bills. All the tips he got in coins went into the coffee cans. After a few years of this, he had a lot of coffee cans.

When approaching friends, coworkers, or family members, the secret to success is to be as organized, formal, and professional in your presentation as if you were pitching the CEO of Chase Bank. It's a grievous error to be as casual about money as you are with other aspects of your relationships with these people. Money is different. You need to go to these people with a thoroughly prepared business plan, deal structure, incentives, and reassurances.

3. Strangers

Personally, I have had great success with finding, meeting, and recruiting strangers as private lenders and investors for my own business ventures as well as my clients'. The biggest advantage of dealing with strangers is that they have no pre-conceived ideas about you.

Dan Kennedy's Eternal Truth #12
Familiarity breeds...

Where do you find strangers to lend or invest? By being active in appropriate trade and business associations, local "lead clubs" and civic activities, and by meeting as many people as possible. Your own networking can lead you to many money sources.

Make yourself visible. Getting publicity for yourself, your products, your ideas, or your business can actually bring money sources out of the woodwork. I know at least three people who, as a result of publicity, had investors calling them, eager to back their projects. When Jeff B. was interviewed for an article published in his city's local business journal about the success of his "singles' seminars," he mentioned his plans for a national network of clubs, seminars, and a publishing business when he was able to find the financing. The following week, he had four people contact him, asking about his plans and financing needs, and one of those subsequently provided $50,000 in capital.

You can also advertise for private lenders or investors. One of the largest retail snack-food chains got its expansion financing as a result of a small classified ad placed by the owner in the *Wall Street Journal*. One client of mine raised $250,000 from five investors, all strangers, all recruited with a classified ad in his city's newspaper.

THE PATCHWORK QUILT

The "big truth" about financing your business is that there will probably not be one single, easy, simple answer to your money needs. Instead, it will probably take a patchwork quilt of sources to get the job done. But anybody who uses lack of capital and the inability to get it as an excuse not to go ahead with a business is just copping out, pure and simple. If you want the money badly enough, you'll get it.

9

KEY PEOPLE FOR YOUR COMPANY

Your friends may come and go, but your enemies accumulate.

Anonymous

TAKING ON PEOPLE FOR THE RIGHT REASONS

Very few people can or want to go it totally alone. Even the Lone Ranger had Tonto. There are many reasons for this urge to surround yourself with others, some good, some not so good.

Some entrepreneurs build up excess staff, for example, out of feelings of insecurity, a feeling that theirs is more of a real business if there are a bunch of employees milling around. Many want associates and employees to counter the stark loneliness of entrepreneurship compared to the camaraderie of a corporate environment. Others need a cheering section. But these are all poor reasons for taking on partners, associates, or employees.

Last year, a client of mine returned home to meet with his accountant after an arduous, week-long business travel adventure. After the meeting, he fired his 14 employees, put his 6,000-square-foot office complex up for lease, and went home to announce to his wife that he was moving his business back into the spare bedroom where it had started a decade before. One year later, he has done about 40% as much gross business as the previous year, but kept more money for himself and his family. And he calculates that the extra hours of work he has to do for himself are offset three-to-one by time saved not dealing with his employees' personal problems, petty disputes with coworkers, and so on.

Of course, not every business lends itself to such dramatic downsizing and simplified operation, but the point remains: too often, entrepreneurs take on people for the wrong reasons.

The right reason to add people to your venture is to contribute to increased profits. There was a time when I would have said that this was the only right reason, but there are others. You may choose, for example, to employ a person who makes your life easier, handles problems for you, and frees up some of your time for personal or family activities, even if, in hard dollars, that person represents expense, not profit. As long as you do that knowingly and deliberately, fine.

The other very good reason is to obtain creativity and experience you cannot provide. Most successful entrepreneurs develop and depend on a small circle of close, trusted associates from their network of partners, key employees, friends, family, even peers, for input, encouragement, and support.

Andrew Carnegie described the formation of such a team as "the master mind concept." The greatest caution that Carnegie, and his protege, Napoleon Hill, had to offer was about choosing the people you include in your master mind group or groups. The need for harmony, these men pointed out, is crucial.

In the entertainment world, a great team of masterminds made the "Tonight Show" an enormously successful television institution: Johnny Carson, Ed McMahon, and producer Fred DeCordova. In the infomercial business, I'm proud to be part of the "brain trust" at Guthy-Renker Corporation that yields successful infomercials such as "Personal Power with Tony Robbins," the "Victoria Principal Skin Care Program," and the *Entrepreneur* magazine show, "Be Your Own Boss." Different Guthy-Renker projects involve different members of a master mind group of about a dozen people including writers, producers, technical people, product development people, and marketing consultants. For my independent productions, I, too, have a pool I draw from for a quality master mind group for each project.

You will no doubt be eager to develop a team of people you can work with in your business. It's important to exercise caution in assembling your team. And you should be very aware of the problems that can arise.

TAKE OFF YOUR ROSE-COLORED GLASSES

Because entrepreneurs tend to be optimists, they generally view people in their best light. But that may be unrealistic and, regrettably, this attitude can lead to frustration more often than to fulfillment. As hard as it may be to understand, some people just do not want to be motivated, to be helped, to be coached, to improve. And, when you try to force it on them, bad things usually happen.

On more than one occasion, I have made the mistake of bringing on a partner with unrealistic expectations. In one case, I brought in a close, personal friend as an executive of a company I had acquired, but I did so without considering the full picture. I saw him as I wanted him to be, not as he really was, and I tried to make him into someone he wasn't prepared to be. The end result was the destruction of a friendship and significant expense to me.

With these experiences under my belt, I've developed some opinions about the special qualifications to look for in key associates.

HOW TO CHOOSE YOUR KEY PEOPLE

Entrepreneurs tend to leap between extremes of refusing to delegate tasks to delegating wildly, sloppily, and hastily. The most important person in the entrepreneur's business life will be very good at running behind, scooping up the pieces, and making sure initiatives get implemented. This key person has to cheerfully accept all this responsibility and, often, read the entrepreneur's mind!

That calls for four strong characteristics:

(a) Ability to accept responsibility

(b) Relatively low need for reassurance and recognition

(c) Ability to cooperate

(d) Ability to confront problems with maturity

This person can't worry about who gets the credit for success or who to blame for mistakes. He or she has to be secure enough about his or her own worth to not need recognition from afar. He or she needs to be very results oriented.

This person also needs to be good at creating and fostering cooperation among others. Because the entrepreneur often moves very quickly and assertively, he or she sometimes runs over other people's sensibilities. Somebody has to clean up that mess, too.

Behind just about every high-profile, highly successful entrepreneur, you'll find several of these key support people. These behind-the-scenes people are much like assistant coaches of major basketball or football teams. The high-profile head coach does the interviews, has the camera's eye, and gets the glory (or the criticism). But that head coach couldn't get through a game without the team of assistant coaches.

85

Last, the entrepreneur's key associate has to have great maturity in his or her handling of problems. This means no panic, no emotional overreactions — just the calm voice of reason. I know several entrepreneurs who have just such people working with them, and they are very fortunate. One real estate broker I know pays his executive secretary $125,000 a year plus perks. Some of the few people who know of this think it's outrageous, but it is good value for what she does — and good business.

IF IT'S NOT MEANT TO BE...

Very few business relationships go the distance. That's why the smartest entrepreneurs develop dissolution agreements at the start of relationships. I know that I will never again take on a partner without such an agreement.

When it becomes evident to you that you have a "cancer" in your business, you cannot afford to hesitate or procrastinate for even a day. Cut out the cancer before it spreads. And this goes double for cancer within your master mind group. If your relationship with a key person deteriorates and there is no hope for recovery, you cannot afford the luxury of keeping that person around.

When you "divorce," do it as decisively, cleanly, and courteously as possible. Avoiding unnecessary animosity is important for many reasons. It's an energy drain. It can block sensible negotiation and settlement. Biting your lip until it bleeds for a few days while getting the person out is infinitely preferable to bleeding for years from vengeful negative attacks. If there's anything reasonable you can do to diffuse the other person's anger, do it. On the other hand, if bloody battle is unavoidable, make it quick. Do what you must do to protect your business.

10
WORKING WITH LAWYERS, ACCOUNTANTS, AND BANKERS

The first thing we do, let's kill all the lawyers.

William Shakespeare, *Henry VI*

The relationships between entrepreneurs and their lawyers, accountants, and bankers tend to be rocky at best. Most entrepreneurs I know harbor intense dislike for these people, including the ones they pay, and all their colleagues. Believe me, I understand this dislike. On the other hand, I have faced the reality that you cannot survive in today's business environment without relationships with these people. It's okay not to like them, but it's still important to try to understand them and to be able to elicit productive results from them.

HOW TO BE LITIGIOUS WITHOUT BUYING YOUR LAWYER A YACHT

I have been accused of being litigious, which means I often threaten to sue and file lawsuits. I have, on a number of occasions, been quick to threaten and quick to proceed; it's often proved to be the best way to avoid being pushed around. I've discovered that most people as well as many companies have no real stomach for legal warfare. They know how costly and time-consuming it can be.

One of the most time-consuming legal weapons is called "discovery." This allows you to subpoena opponents' records, interrogate them under oath, and serve them with written interrogatories that must be completed within a certain period of time. An interrogatory is a written set of questions, pages long, prying into every imaginable aspect of the opponent's business and personal life. If there is a possibility of your being awarded damages from your lawsuit, you have the right to discover, in advance, the nature and location of all the opponent's assets. You can ask for detailed information about income, bank accounts, and personal and family assets.

With this approach, you can consume immense amounts of the opponent's time and force public disclosure of information he or she would rather not make public. Also, dropping a 200-page interrogatory on an opponent's spouse can make for a very interesting evening in their home. Used properly, the firing of the interrogatory is often the only shot you have to fire.

In a number of conflicts, people have instantly become more reasonable and respectful as soon as they've realized that I was prepared to bring in the legal beagles and start discovery. I signify this by sending copies to my lawyer of the correspondence I have with the other party, and, sometimes copying that party my memo to my lawyer. Using only this method, I've settled in my favor of a lot of problems.

Just recently, for example, I used this method to settle a dispute with a trade magazine that had made a mistake with the photos in an advertisement we placed. When the magazine billed us $1,800, I wrote to the publisher expressing my dissatisfaction. When that got nowhere, I sent a second letter indicating my refusal to pay any amount and describing how the deficient ad had probably damaged us at a trade show. I then sent a copy of the letter to my lawyer. Soon afterward, I got an offer from the publisher to settle for $900. I counter-offered, again sending a copy of the letter to my lawyer, and settled for $500.

Why, you ask, did I do all the work myself? Why not just turn it over to the lawyers from the beginning?

First of all, although some of my companies have had lawyers on retainer, I do not now have a blanket retainer arrangement. Carbon-copying costs me nothing. Having a lawyer handle it costs me $150 an hour. Second, I wanted to rattle my sabers, not actually wind up in battle.

Keep in mind that your interests and your lawyer's interests rarely coincide. In matter of the $1,800 bill I describe above, I would have had to nudge, push, and check up on the lawyer a half-dozen times to get it handled. Lawyers tend to deal each day with only those matters that have escalated to crisis, so a case like mine could have been put on the back burner forever. It would have cost me more than the $1,300 that I saved to get it done.

Using a similar threat of litigation, I have, at various times, stopped a competitive company's salesperson from spreading rumors, got an insurance company to pay off nearly $250,000 in claims on a technically lapsed policy, got an undesirable equipment lease terminated without penalty, reduced and compromised bills, and collected past-due balances.

My objective through all this is to win cheaply and quickly. And, in 25-odd years of using this approach, I've wound up in actual lawsuits only four times: settling twice and litigating twice.

YOUR TURN CAN COME

I am not the only litigious soul on earth. It comes as a seismic shock to many entrepreneurs how easily and frequently they can be threatened with lawsuits. Anybody can sue you at anytime for anything. Sure, you have recourse in most cases where the suit filed against you proves baseless, and you can demonstrate cash damages as a result. By that time, though, you've had your business and family disrupted, tied up money in legal fees and costs, and consumed a fortune in antacids.

When you get attacked, most lawyers will want to react and proceed slowly, cautiously, and by the book. I've found, however, that when threatened or served with a lawsuit, the best defense is a very fast, very strong, even a little wild-eyed-and-foaming-at-the-mouth, kick-butt offense. Push your lawyer to run straight at them.

While responding with your own attack, stay calm. Nothing really happens very quickly in 90% of the legal disputes. Paper goes back and forth with long delays in between. You have plenty of time to think, research, develop strategy, negotiate, and solve the problems. This battle has plenty of time-outs.

Legal problems are a part of business. The old idea that nobody has legal problems unless they deserve them is as out-of-date as handshake agreements and leaving the back door unlocked while you take an evening stroll down to the ice cream parlor.

Dan Kennedy's Eternal Truth #13
Talk is cheap...until you hire a lawyer.

WHEN YOU MUST REALLY USE A LAWYER

Keep this in mind: don't lose control. Don't be intimidated. Don't let yourself leave with a pat on the head, a reassuring word, and unanswered questions. You must understand everything about your situation. Take nothing for granted. Insist on being an informed participant in the strategy process. If the lawyer wants to tell you what to do rather than educate you about your options and their ramifications and help you make your decision, run.

You must manage your lawyer just as you would any other employee. Be very clear about fees, costs, and how the relationship is to work. Follow up on every phone conversation or meeting with a written letter, "just to confirm what we agreed to do," and use this memo to reference and enforce deadlines. Be polite and considerate, of course, but firm. You are the boss — act like it.

Some lawyers will work effectively with you in this kind of a relationship. Some will not. There are plenty to choose from.

If you feel a complaint against your lawyer is in order, your city's Bar Association office (in the United States) or Law Society (in Canada) will give you a booklet about filing complaints and forms to use for that purpose. They get a lot of "nut case complaints," so, if you do file your complaint, it's important to make it very articulate, very calmly thought out, very unemotional, and very thorough. Often, just threatening to complain or preparing the complaint and plopping it on the lawyer's desk is enough.

The filing of such a complaint against your own lawyer or against an adversary's lawyer is your prerogative. There are many possible reasons for a complaint: negligence, refusal to communicate, incompetence, violation of the Fair Credit Act in collection activity, even failure to properly advise you of all options available to you.

ACCOUNTANTS

Accountants can be almost as maddening as lawyers to the entrepreneur, but for different reasons. The temperament and thinking of someone happy to sit in an office crunching numbers all day is diametrically opposed to the personality of the go-get-'em entrepreneur.

Still, you need a good accountant.

What is a good accountant? The entrepreneurial joke is that you ask "What's this number?" and the good accountant says, "What would you like it to be?" That's amusing right up until the first tax audit or visit from some tax authority. My own working definition, which may or may not be exactly right for you, is that a good accountant imposes a reasonable degree of discipline on your record keeping and is very knowledgeable, informative, and helpful in the area of tax law — where your biggest risks and biggest costs can occur.

You can learn to do basic bookkeeping yourself, either manually or using accounting software on your computer.

BANKERS

You should realize right off the bat that the entire banking system is geared to dealing with salaried employees who regularly and consistently deposit their paychecks, settle for minimum interest on their savings, get home mortgage and car loans, and make few demands. In contrast to these customers, entrepreneurs are a nuisance. The entrepreneur has many of the same needs as the huge corporate depositor, but lacks the "weight."

Here are some steps you can take to make working with banks easier:

(a) *Recognize banks and bankers for what they are.* Harbor no illusions that yours is different, that your banker is your ally. Everything may be fine as long as everything's fine and you don't ask for much.

(b) *Do the best you can to build and maintain good relationships.* It's not going to get you much, but it can get you a little extra cooperation once in a while, and that might make an important difference one day.

(c) *Don't expect bankers to think like businesspeople.* Understand their concerns and avoid doing things that will add to that concern. Keep them informed of positive progress of your business in neat, concise ways, so they can easily understand what you are telling them. If your business is unusual or diversified, you will have to simplify for the banker's sake.

(d) *Forget privacy.* Anything the bank knows, the world can easily know, too.

(e) *Keep accounts in more than one bank.* Because a bank can freeze, seize, or close your accounts at a moment's notice, for its own reasons or for the benefit of a creditor or government agency, it's very unwise to have all your eggs in one bank's basket. As your business grows, you'll want to separate funds into at least two different institutions, maybe more, possibly with one of them out of your home area. It's also smart to do your personal banking at a different institution than your business banking. Many entrepreneurs prefer to split their businesses into several different corporations as another means of protection.

(f) *Do your very best to avoid "negative account activity."* This includes overdrafting your account as well as depositing others' checks that are returned for insufficient funds — the bank will judge you based on the bad behavior of your customers.

WHO CAN YOU COUNT ON?

In all of these necessary relationships, strive to make things the best they can be, but do everything you can to insure against them turning to the worst they can be. The only person you can completely rely on to protect your interests is you.

11

WHY ENTREPRENEURS AREN'T MANAGERS — AND WHAT YOU CAN DO ABOUT IT

Never try to teach a pig to sing. You'll only annoy the pig and get yourself covered with mud.

Unknown

I feel fortunate that for most of my life I have operated businesses with a minimum number of employees. Today, I have a small team including family and a couple that have been with me so long they seem like family. But, at one point, I suddenly took over a company with 43 employees. The old management had been dictatorial and ineffective. There were massive quality control, productivity, and other problems. It was a hostile environment. I determined to do something about all that.

At the time, I had been doing a massive amount of reading about different management styles: Japanese management, open-door management, management by objectives, management by values, team-building, and building ownership mentality. Exciting buzzwords, all of them. Once again, however, I discovered that most of the folks writing these theories never managed anybody. Or they managed only in their memories, from a time when people latched onto a good job and then did everything in their power to keep it; when getting sacked was a red badge of humiliation. Times are different now.

So, I waded in with all this terrific theory and got my head handed back to me, with bloody claw marks all over it. I sewed it back on, stuck it in there again, and pulled out a bloody stump.

What have I learned from that experience and from working with clients beset with management problems? The big secret. And here it is: all the theories work wonderfully with wonderful people. But trying to teach pigs to sing or chickens to soar is tough, tough sledding.

For example, I do a lot of consulting work with chiropractors. Typically, they have staffs of three to ten people who are all very important. Their contact with patients affects repeat business and referrals. Their attitudes affect the doctor's attitude, and these practices are attitude-driven businesses. I know doctors who bring their entire staffs to seminars, and there they are, smiling, happy, enthusiastic people, eager to do their jobs better. These doctors have incentive and bonus programs for their staffs. They set and work on team goals. They really have a team effort going. I also know doctors who have to pay and coerce their staffs to grudgingly come to a seminar. And there they are, stiff, frowning, restless, ants-in-their-pants, in and out of the room. These doctors try incentive and bonus programs and they fail miserably. If these doctors try to talk "teamwork," the staff members mutter "He's been to another seminar. It'll all blow over in a few days."

Using exactly the same management ideas, philosophies, methods, and strategies, one doctor will get incredibly good results; the other will be cut off at the knees.

Which brings us to several really tough, no B.S. management principles.

YOU CAN'T TEACH A PIG TO SING

I repeat it again. You can apply the very same sound, proven motivational tools to ten people and get ten startlingly different results. Perhaps, theoretically, everybody and anybody can change and can be inspired to change, but many "hard cases" just aren't worth the investment, as a practical matter.

HIRE SLOW, FIRE FAST

This motto hangs on the wall of the CEO of one of the four largest chains of weight-loss centers. But this philosophy is, of course, the exact opposite of what entrepreneurs tend to do. We hate to fire anybody. We're optimists, so we believe that everybody can be saved. We keep trying, we keep giving them one more chance. By the time we finally fire them, they walk away wondering why it took us so long. Our other staff members wonder why it took so long.

Then, we have this vacuum to fill. We need that work done. So, we grab the first warm body who passes by. And, as they say, you have to kiss a lot of frogs to find a prince. I've gone through over 55 people to get 4 good ones. Am I inept? Well, most entrepreneurs I know who get to have a good team behind them, get there by hiring, firing, hiring, firing, catching and throwing them back, and only very occasionally finding a "keeper."

FORGET THE IDEA OF OWNERSHIP MENTALITY

Listen, the only people who have ownership mentality are owners. That's that. Why should it be any other way? The main reason that managing people drives entrepreneurs crazy is all our silly, stubborn hopes, beliefs, and assumptions that "they" are like "us." They're not. If they were, they wouldn't be working for us — they'd be competing with us.

I have achieved a new peace of mind in recent years by recalibrating my expectations for the performance of different people in different positions. Each position has different responsibilities and different definitions of satisfactory performance and of excellent performance, and, in most cases, these positions do not require another you to meet these definitions.

I have two employees, for example, who just aren't "morning people." For years, it drove me bananas that they could not get to work on time. It drove a business partner of mine right over the edge. It became his mission to end their tardiness; he tried everything and failed. Otherwise, however, these two are exemplary employees. You couldn't ask for better team members. They perfectly fulfill the performance requirements of their positions. They're not duplicates of me, and they do not need to be.

A couple of years ago, we arrived at a big breakthrough. We made a new deal. We told these two they could come and go and work pretty much whenever they wanted to work as long as all the work that needs to get done is done on time. Now, if they meander in at 9:45 a.m., nobody thinks anything of it. I don't even ask or pay any attention to when they're there and when they're not. I have wiped an entire chunk of anxiety and aggravation right off my plate.

But, make no mistake about it, they only excel at meeting reasonable expectations for their positions. They're not me. And no one, and I mean no one, will ever care about the quality, accuracy, or effectiveness of their work as much as I have to. That's just the way it is.

Dan Kennedy's Eternal Truth #14
No one will ever care about your business
as much as you do.

YOU CAN ONLY EXPECT WHAT YOU INSPECT

This is an old management axiom and you've probably heard it before. Well, truth is truth, and if you want to stay sane, this is the way to manage.

Business owners don't want to believe their employees steal from them. Some don't even track their losses, they just stick their heads in the sand. And they're all wrong, because most employees steal at some time.

About 2% of the population are incapable of ever stealing; they would rather starve. Another 2% will steal for a nickel; they are incapable of being honest. The remaining 96% of people will steal if three factors are present:

(a) need,

(b) ability to rationalize their actions, and

(c) opportunity to get away with it.

You cannot control the first two factors. Ask your employees if they need more money or if they need to take shortcuts in their work (another form of stealing), and most will answer yes. And most of us are pretty good at rationalizing our behavior. It often is expressed with words like "He just bought a new hot car and lives high on the hog. We do all the dirty work around here — he'll never miss a few dollars. And he deserves to be nailed anyway."

However, you can control opportunity, and that is why you can only expect what you inspect.

I took over a custom products manufacturing company once with a serious quality-control problem. Over 30% of all jobs had something wrong with them. In one month, that dropped to 5%. How did I do it? I simply took the time to walk around the plant at different times, almost every day, randomly pulling samples out of production and checking them. As soon as everybody knew that the risk of detection was high, the error rate dropped.

This isn't rocket science; it's simple. It's applicable to any business.

IDENTIFY, KEEP, REWARD, AND MOTIVATE

Mike Vance, one of the top executives of the Disney corporation for a number of years and now a management consultant, says that management is all about "developing people through work, while having fun."

I agree with him — I'm not a cynic after all! I believe that smart entrepreneur-managers provide environments, opportunities, and encouragement for growth to whatever degree is possible. I believe sensitivity toward the non-monetary rewards of work is important. And I believe in having fun and offering bonuses, incentives, team goals, compete-against-yourselves contests, and, of course, an overall positive attitude.

In all business, unhappy people do poor work. It is part of good management to create the right environment in the workplace. You will, in the long term, be rewarded for bringing this kind of positive environment into your workplace. There are people out there who would kill for an opportunity to work in a good job, for somebody who respects and appreciates them, who lets them grow with authority and responsibility, and who includes them in a team effort.

Quality people respond to quality management techniques, so you'll be involved in going through people, weeding out the uncooperative, identifying the gems, keeping, developing, involving, and rewarding the keepers. Because everything is always changing — people, their circumstances, your business, and you — this process will continue as long as you remain at the helm, so you must accept and understand it. Don't resent it, and do it as effectively as you can.

WHAT WORKS FOR YOU IS WHAT'S RIGHT

Throw out the textbooks.

Five of the most successful CEOs I know have five dramatically different management styles. Their relationships with their people are different. Their beliefs about leadership are different. Their companies' environments feel different when you walk in. There *is* more than one right way.

Harold Geneen, who led the giant ITT, once said, "I have never come across a chief executive who tried, much less succeeded, running his company according to any set formula, chart, or business theory."

This is my most important message in this chapter on management: my way, that works for me, may very well fail miserably for you. You have to find your own way.

12
HOW TO MANAGE YOUR CASH FLOW

I've got plenty of money to last the rest of my life, as long as I don't want to buy anything or go anywhere.

Unknown

It's amazing what you can do with cash. There have been times in my entrepreneurial career when as little as a few thousand dollars of cash could have made a million-dollar difference. I once saved a million-dollar business from extinction with $25,000.

Dan Kennedy's Eternal Truth #15
Cash is king.

Happiness is positive cash flow. Many businesses struggle through years of losses before achieving profitability, but survive thanks to positive cash flow. In business, cash flow buys the extra time necessary to win. Cash flow provides the staying power needed to invent, experiment, sort it all out, and, finally, wind up with a winning system. It's not all that unusual for one new product, one new ad, or one sales breakthrough to swing a company from losing to winning. To outsiders, it may look like a lucky miracle. Actually, it's the logical result of a progression of experiments, failures, corrections, decisions, investments, and actions.

Over the years, I've developed methods for increasing cash flow regardless of other aspects of a business. I call these my MCF methods: multiplied cash flow methods.

THE FIVE KEYS TO MULTIPLIED CASH FLOW

1. How to reduce and control expenses

Most businesses have an incredible capacity to accumulate fat when the owners aren't looking. Phone bills, freight costs, office-supply expenses, shrinkage — all sorts of expenses can creep up.

To stay on top of it all, you should know what your gross sales need to be in relation to each category of expense. You can determine these ratios by finding out what the norms are for your business or industry from your trade associations, reading reference materials, and relying on your own business experience. For example, let's say that in your business, long-distance phone costs should be between 5% and 7% of gross sales. Each month you run your own calculation. If this month it comes up 11%, you have reason to be alarmed.

It's not my nature to pinch pennies, but I've learned that controlling expenses is another way of making money, no less important than any other. If in your business, it takes, on average, $4 of sales to put $1 at the bottom line, it takes $4,000 to yield $1,000. That means $1,000 saved is the same as $4,000 sold.

2. How to get financing leverage

Obviously, the longer you can delay payments, the longer you have the use of that money. Big companies routinely take 60 or 90 days to pay their bills, and get away with it because of their size. They use that "float" to make money. The small entrepreneur needs to keep this in mind and delay payments whenever possible without damaging credit ratings. Here are a few tips:

- Never pay bills early. Incredibly, many entrepreneurs do. If they ever do have a cash crunch, this pattern will be to their detriment. Their creditors will be spoiled and judge them more harshly. Pay on time, but never early. Paying early is a dangerous precedent to set.

- Negotiate extended terms in advance with suppliers. Many entrepreneurs are pleasantly surprised at how easily this can be done. Vendors competing for your business will use financing to get it. Instead of terms of "net 30 days," you may be able to negotiate paying in 2 or 3 installments, like a third in 30 days, a third in 60 days, and a third in 90 days.

- Conserve cash by leasing with deferred balloon payments.

- Refinance when you don't have to, to consolidate debt and reduce monthly debt service.

- If you have financed your business start-up with personal collateral and guarantees and a patchwork quilt of financing sources, strive to replace that with conventional business loans and lines of credit, secured by the business, as soon as you can. With two years of profitability, growth, and a good payment track record, you can start working on this aggressively, shopping among banks if necessary.

3. How to get paid

Many businesses suffer from some or all of the following credit-management deficiencies:

(a) Loose credit policies

(b) No credit checks before granting credit

103

(c) No enforcement of credit limits

(d) Late invoicing

(e) Credit given to those with past-due balances

(f) No standardized collection procedures

(g) Unwillingness to get tough

If you are going to grant credit, you need to have a plan to prevent problems and resolve them when they do occur. Making sales doesn't matter much if you don't get paid. Take the following steps to implement your plan:

(a) Develop strict credit policies.

(b) Make each customer complete a credit application.

(c) Check the references.

(d) Consider joining a credit bureau and checking credit files.

(e) Set credit limits for each customer.

(f) Send your invoices out promptly.

(g) Implement a collection procedure beginning with the first of three warning notices out the 32nd day.

(h) Cut off past-due clients, and only then negotiate a "deal" as you see fit. Do not keep granting credit to people who cannot or will not pay you.

(i) Get tough when you have to. Preserving the goodwill of a customer who can't or won't pay is silly.

This is all common sense, isn't it? So why do so many entrepreneurs do such lousy jobs of collecting the money owed them? Because while wearing one hat, trying to negotiate with their vendors to get better terms, they develop great empathy for their customers. They find it difficult to switch attitudes when they switch hats.

For more good ideas on collecting techniques, see *Collect Those Debts!*, another title in the Self-Counsel Series.

4. Increase cash flow by increasing sales

Most entrepreneurs would argue that increasing sales is the first step to increasing cash flow. But sales alone aren't the answer. Driving up sales without a thorough approach to cash flow management and profit management will wind up enriching everybody but you. You'll need more people, more equipment, more inventory, more freight, more postage, etc., and everyone will get richer — but will you?

Sometimes, it's even helpful to cut back sales volume, cut out the least profitable product lines or parts of a business, and alter the economics for the better — much like pruning a bush so it can grow straighter and stronger.

5. How to find or invent a "slack adjuster"

Those in the used car business use the term "slack adjuster" to describe the occasional great buy they find somewhere, like a ten-year-old car in mint condition that they buy for $500 and can sell for $2,000. This kind of sale far exceeds their normal mark-up.

A "slack adjuster" is something you sell that gives you a surge of extra profit to help pick up the slack.

In the travel business, full-fare air tickets, first-class seats, and packages can be slack adjusters. In the appliance business, it's the add-on warranties they sell. In the finance business, it's "credit life insurance" — probably the worst insurance buy ever perpetrated on consumers.

Through some or all of these methods you can multiply and maximize your business's cash flow, and, as a result, give yourself every possible opportunity to win big.

13
HOW TO PREVAIL

*No one ever would have crossed the
ocean if he could have gotten off the
ship in the storm.*

C.F. Kettering

When it comes to success, the determination to prevail far
outshadows talent, genius, and education in importance. For
the entrepreneur, there is no one to hand a letter of resignation
to when the going gets tough. The single most important
characteristic I've observed common to all successful entrepreneurs is the refusal to be broken.

HOW TOUGH ARE YOU?

Anger. Frustration. Resentment. Depression. Grief. Fear.

An entrepreneur can't get a divorce from these human
emotions. The difference between entrepreneurs and other
people is the amount of time and energy given up to these
emotions.

Most people are immobilized when these feelings hit.
They move from one destructive emotional state to another.
When the entrepreneur experiences these feelings, he or she
learns to quickly get through them, then get back on track and
stay focused on positive goals and productive activities.

Do I get angry? You bet! I get angry at staff, at associates, family members, vendors, clients, and government.

Am I resentful? I resent disloyalty, ingratitude, lying, and scheming.

Am I frustrated? For years, I was frustrated by severely limited resources, the criminal stupidity of some bankers, and the incompetence of some lawyers.

Was I depressed? I wonder how many times I've thought very seriously of getting out of business altogether and taking an easier, less stressful job. Grief? Yes, over lost opportunities, dissolved friendships.

Frightened? You can't lose a major account, face a five-figure bank overdraft, or walk into a courtroom for a legal battle and not be afraid.

Dan Kennedy's Eternal Truth #16
The entrepreneurial experience is going to challenge you at the very core of your being. At least once, you will want to quit.

Entrepreneurship has been glamorized in the media. TV programs like the old "Designing Women" or "Newhart" programs, for example, showed their lead characters who are self-employed hanging out, having fun, never under any time pressure, and rarely even seen doing any work, let along worrying about an upcoming payroll.

Are there "Happy Days" like these? Of course. There are times when there is more freedom, fun, excitement, achievement, and sheer, unadulterated, childish joy than you can imagine. But there are also bad days.

Make no mistake about this: entrepreneurship is a survival test without comparison, and you are going to do battle with an incredible number of forces, including your own emotions.

THE BATTLES YOU'LL FIGHT WITH YOURSELF

Business isn't like a football game with immediate results on the scoreboard. You can take action today and not have it proven right or wrong for months — even years. You can go days or weeks without being able to see any clear, measurable progress. All of this can take a tough emotional toll and it can foster self-doubt. The biggest battle you'll fight with yourself, though, will occur when you fail. I mean clearly, inarguably fail.

Dan Kennedy's Eternal Truth #17
How you deal with failure determines whether or not you ever get the opportunity to deal with success.

Research supervised by a professor at Tulane University's School of Business revealed that the average entrepreneur goes through 3.8 failures before achieving significant success. If you study the lives of past and present successful entrepreneurs, you may be surprised how many of them suffered business failures, bankruptcies, and humiliation before putting the pieces together the right way. You might say that behind every great entrepreneurial success is an embarrassing entrepreneurial failure.

I've come to the conclusion that the way you deal with failure controls your future opportunities to deal with success. In fact, it is through failure that you learn to overcome the fear of failure! And once experience demonstrates that failure isn't fatal, you can move on, full steam ahead.

Some people, when they experience failure, give up trying altogether. Others bury themselves in guilt. Maybe they have lost some investor's money or let their family or friends down. They use every bad decision and every ineffective plan to build a very heavy bat, then they beat themselves into the ground with it.

An entrepreneur has to acknowledge and understand these common responses to failure, then control and manage them, and refocus on positive goals. The entrepreneur has to learn the difference between responsibility and guilt, between business failures and personal failures.

Consider the CEO of a major television network who is ultimately responsible for all the programming. He or she has to decide what new program ideas have promise and which do not, approve budgets for new shows, and invest millions. These new shows are then highly publicized, but there are always some among them that don't work out. In fact, in popular television, most of the projects are losers.

Think of the CEO of an auto manufacturing company who approves a line of new car designs. He or she approves perhaps two dozen, multi-million-dollar ad campaigns in a year. Some sell well; others fail.

What about the CEO of a national bank? He or she loans and invests money. Some deals go bad.

These people cannot and usually do not give up on themselves and quit their businesses. They don't fold up and roll under the bed never to be seen again. Life goes on.

You're going to make some mistakes, too. These mistakes will seem even more earthshaking because there's no big corporation to absorb them, no place to hide. Some corporate CEOs can make million-dollar mistakes and barely feel the effect. You might make a $10,000 mistake and sink your business.

You *must* limit your feelings of responsibility for your entrepreneurial errors and failures. Yes, you should behave responsibly, but you cannot absorb an unlimited amount of guilt either. Guilt is warranted only if your intentions were dishonorable.

THE BATTLES YOU'LL FIGHT WITH OTHERS

One of the most frustrating aspects of being an entrepreneur is how much time, energy, and effort you invest in winning battles you shouldn't have to fight in the first place — and winning the same battle over and over again. I believe that the reason this happens is because almost every industry and company in North America today has become infested with massive incompetence.

There are dozens of examples of this kind of battle: fighting for proper service on a photocopying system you just bought; following up on "lost" orders from vendors; correcting bank errors; etc. I have never found a way to eliminate this kind of "fighting to get it right" from business. However, I have developed a few ideas to handle it better:

(a) Clearly communicate your expectations to everyone with whom you interact. In most cases, that means *put it in writing.*

(b) Instill a sense of urgency in your staff. Employees will often accept excuses or even sympathize with your vendors' employees or repair technicians, for example. Your staff must understand that every minute a

110

problem goes unresolved costs the company money, and that their job, as a member of your team, is to demand and get fast and correct responses.

(c) Resist letting others transfer their problems to you. This is a big self-defense principle for the beleaguered entrepreneur. If the vendor's employee is absent, the truck has broken down, they are unusually busy today, or a storm hit town, that is their problem, not yours. There is no acceptable excuse for non-performance. Believe me, your customers aren't going to accept excuses from you, and you shouldn't from your vendors. If someone throws their problems at you, throw them back.

(d) Don't hesitate to get tough when you have to. You've heard that you can get more done with a kind word and a smile. Al Capone said "you can get even more done with a kind word, a smile, and a gun." I wish it weren't so, but nine times out of ten, it pays to be firm, then get tough fast. Tolerance and patience isn't going to help if your business's success is on the line, threatened by others' incompetence.

(e) Never accept anyone's contention that nothing more can be done. Something can always be done. The question is, what will it take to get it done? One time we had some very costly and essential typesetting equipment malfunctioning because of errors made by the service technicians. At 5:00 p.m., they blithely announced that there was nothing more they could do and they had to leave to catch an airplane. I told them that they had to stay, and I locked them in the room and disconnected the phones at the switchboard. At first, they thought I was kidding, but soon realized I meant business. Four hours later, my equipment was running perfectly.

111

YOU WILL BE TESTED

It is always a shock the first time you are sued, or the first time you are stabbed in the back by a trusted employee, or the first time you run against a bureaucratic foe. Most entrepreneurs, being the optimists they are, never think that these barriers will be put in front of them.

I don't know a single successful entrepreneur with over ten years in business who hasn't been sued or run into problems with governments. The typical entrepreneur faces new tests every day. Some are easy, but every once in a while you are faced with a real challenge — a problem big enough to destroy you. When that happens, how will you respond?

The answer to that will be the measure of your success.

14
HOW TO ACHIEVE PEAK PRODUCTIVITY

The hurrieder I go, the behinder I get.

Pennsylvania Dutch saying

As a teenager, I worked summers as a groom at a harness racetrack, taking care of horses and shoveling manure. A lot of manure. Every workday started at 5:00 a.m., stopped around 1:00 p.m., started back up about 5:00 p.m. to get the horses that were racing that night ready, and finished after the races, 9:00, 10:00, or 11:00 p.m.

During the day, I worked in aluminum-roofed barns that absorbed the sun's heat and cooked us pretty well. I filled wicker baskets with manure, about two per stall, anywhere from three to a dozen stalls, hauled the baskets the length of the barn, hoisted them up, and emptied them into the manure wagons. I fed, watered, and groomed the horses. I worked on their sore legs and feet. I walked them. I stacked bales of straw and hay.

All of it was hard work. Looking back, I have fondness and nostalgia for it all. But it was hard, hard work.

But, no matter how hard you have worked in previous jobs, you'll discover that running your business is even harder, more intense work. The pace and pressure of being the person in charge is unlike any other, and it requires masterful organization, control, and use of time. It requires that you have the ability to do many things at once. The multiple demands on the entrepreneur's time are extraordinary, and you need extraordinary measures to match these demands.

Time is the most valuable asset any entrepreneur possesses. Time to step aside and think. Time to network. Time to solve problems. Time to invent sales and marketing breakthroughs. *The use or misuse of your time — the degree with which you achieve peak productivity — will determine your success as an entrepreneur.*

Dan Kennedy's Eternal Truth #19
There is never enough time (or enough
of any other resource, for that matter).
Entrepreneurs learn to get what they want
working with what they've got.

Time may be the biggest problem in business, and the biggest societal concern of the 1990s. The Fortune 500 companies spend millions annually on time management training and productivity analysis. The market is clogged with time management systems and seminars. Despite all this, most businesspeople I know are still woefully disorganized, behind in their work, running faster and faster to try to catch up. One research study I read about some years ago concluded that the average corporate CEO actually logs less than 90 minutes a day of genuinely productive time. I don't doubt it. And I suggest entrepreneurs have even bigger problems with time.

Imagine — in an 8- to 10-hour workday, being able to count just 90 minutes of it as productive! Clearly, you can give yourself a tremendous competitive advantage if you can make more of your time productive.

WHY IS TIME SUCH A PROBLEM?

Let me make it clear that I do *not* claim to be the most organized entrepreneur around. Most people marvel at how much I am able to accomplish, and I seem to be able to handle more responsibilities than many people, but I really fight to maintain the level of organization I've got. Once or twice a year, I have to set aside a few days to strip files, discard accumulated piles of miscellaneous material, and get freshly organized. I'm always striving for even a minute-a-day improvement in productivity because I know how that can be leveraged into wealth.

To achieve peak productivity, you've got to know what it is, and when you're hitting it — and when you're not. Most people have no clue. Most people work harder and faster, "systemizing" without the ability to determine whether they're really getting anywhere.

I have devoted quite a bit of thought to defining what productivity really is — and what it isn't. The definition for peak productivity that I've developed is:

> The use of your time, energy, intelligence, resources, and opportunities in a manner calculated to move you measurably closer to meaningful goals.

Once you understand and accept this definition, you'll be better able to choose what to do, what to delegate, and what to leave undone.

WHY "DO IT NOW" MAY NOT BE
THE BEST ADVICE

The favorite affirmation of self-made multi-millionaire and success expert W. Clement Stone is "Do it now!" Given that something should be done, and should be done by you, then "Do it now!" is good advice. Procrastination is insidious.

But many people erroneously accept the do-it-now idea as a prison sentence requiring them to try and do *everything* now. Some things shouldn't be done now. Some things should be deliberately assigned to next week or next month. Some things shouldn't be done at all. And, the busier I am and the older I get, the more I conclude that the greatest wisdom of all is in astutely choosing what *not* to bother with.

It's interesting how obligated most people feel to answer a ringing phone. They'll interrupt whatever they are doing to pick up the receiver, even if they are in the shower! When somebody calls the office and leaves a message, people feel obligated to call back, even when they don't know the caller!

The same is true for letters. When people receive letters in the office, they feel obligated to reply. Because someone appears in the office doorway, we feel obligated to acknowledge them, to invite them in, to talk with them. And on and on.

It bewilders a lot of people that I, for example, will go days without checking my phone messages or opening my mail. And, at home, I'll often take the phone off the hook for hours to write, nap, watch a game, whatever. "Having that phone off the hook would drive me crazy," a friend said. "I'd be worrying the whole time about who might be trying to call me."

I think you have to shake off the shackles of ordinary and customary obligations and feel free to do whatever assists you in achieving peak productivity.

THE YES OR NO TEST

These days, when someone asks me to do something, attend a meeting, talk with somebody, read something, whatever, I silently ask myself: Is this going to move me measurably closer to a goal? If not, I do my best to say no.

I think in terms of investing time. After all, if time is money, then you must either be spending or investing it. Would you knowingly invest your money in, say, a stock that promised no dividends? No. You might choose to spend some money on things offering no monetary profit such as tickets to the theater, flowers for your spouse, or a vacation. In proper balance, this kind of spending is healthy. But investing time in activities unlikely to pay any kind of dividend is stupid. You must be very astute at making these time-investment decisions.

So, always ask yourself, Is this demand on my time a wise investment? Yes or no?

WHAT NOW?

One of the classic problems faced by new entrepreneurs is the absence of an imposed work plan. As someone else's employee, a work plan is imposed on you by your employer. Your adherence to that plan may be policed by managers and supervisors. You are held accountable for effectiveness in adhering to and accomplishing that plan. Deviations from the imposed plan are restricted, sometimes punished. That imposed plan causes you to behave in a disciplined fashion. For example, you get up at a certain time every morning to arrive at work at a set, acceptable time. Maybe you get all your expense reports in order every Thursday afternoon because you are expected to submit them on Friday. You get your monthly newsletter out to your customers because that's part of the imposed plan.

Now you're an entrepreneur. You are your own boss — you can smash that alarm clock with a sledge hammer and set your own hours. You decide what will be done, when and how.

But for many new entrepreneurs, when they get free of the job, they don't know what to do next. It's too much freedom. They wind up paralyzed, looking around for somebody to tell them what to do.

You have to set up your own work plan. I am most productive when I operate under a self-imposed work plan that creates at least as much discipline as any employer-imposed plan would — preferably more. You have to be tough on yourself and set deadlines. If you wouldn't accept an excuse from someone working for you, you can't accept it from yourself. If you're trying to set an example of leadership for others around you, you have to overdo it: be more organized than they need to be, be more punctual than they need to be.

Last year, I wrote two books for bookstore distribution, four other books for mail-order distribution, and several audio programs. I edited two monthly newsletters and did direct-response copywriting for clients. If I wrote only when I felt like it, when I was inspired, when the time was right, I'd be finishing last year's workload in my next life. No, I wrote when I was tired, when I was uninspired, when I was too busy, not just in my office but on airplanes and in hotel rooms. I put myself under self-imposed work plans and deadlines to create discipline.

Nobody's going to do this for you. You're on your own.

Another prevalent problem entrepreneurs fight in achieving peak productivity is other people's disrespect for time. Most people don't value their time very highly, and, as a result, don't place much value on yours either. Given half a chance, most of the people around you will waste your time.

In recent years, I've become militant about guarding my time. I've learned, for example, not to set up business meetings in restaurants. If I'm going to a business lunch with someone, I'll have them first come to my office. When you arrange to meet people in restaurants, you waste a lot of time waiting for them because very few people are punctual. If they're late but they're coming to your office, productivity can continue until they arrive.

I also have my incoming calls carefully screened. This does occasionally irritate people, but that only serves notice to me that the irritated person is not a very successful businessperson. He or she may be able to afford to waste time; I can't. So, in my office, no calls are put through nor are any messages even accepted unless the caller fully identifies himself or herself and the reasons for calling. My best guess is that there are a dozen callers a day who do not get through to me and never will, because they refuse to identify themselves. Even at just three minutes a call, that alone saves me 36 minutes a day.

My staff encourages people to send or fax me brief, introductory notes before trying to get on the phone with me. Many times, others can handle these matters and I'm not needed at all.

PUT A STAKE THROUGH THE HEART OF EVERY "TIME VAMPIRE" WHO COMES YOUR WAY

Time vampires are people who seem dedicated to wasting your time. They're out to suck up *all* of your time. In the process, they also suck out a lot of your energy, leaving you white, weak, and behind schedule. These are the repetitive, frequent drop-in visitors. The employee whose favorite phrase is, "Have you got a minute?" Or they're infused with "meeting-itis." They're chronically disorganized. Each time one of these vampires drops by and hangs out, picture him or her sinking teeth into your neck and sucking out a pint or two.

Suppose, for example, you want to make $100,000 this year, which means your work hour is worth about $36, which is about 60 cents a minute. So when a time vampire sucks about 20 minutes in a meeting for something that could have been handled with a 4-minute phone call, that person just sucked over $9 right out of your wallet. If that happens 5 times in a week, you lose $45. Over 50 weeks, that's $2,250.

THE SECRET OF SECRETS OF GETTING RICH

Perhaps you think I'm overdoing this — beating this drum too loudly. But let me tell you why it's impossible to over-emphasize the deliberate achievement of peak productivity. It is the secret of secrets to getting rich.

Exceptional success in any business is the result of strategically directing ever-increasing amounts of your time to the activities you're very good at and very excited about. When you start a business, you do it all. The trick is to stay at that stage as briefly as possible, and, as you grow out of it to grow by directing increasing amounts of your time to those aspects of the business you have the most passion for and do best.

You can never make this happen if your time is being abused, wasted, lost, sucked up by vampires, and controlled by everybody but you.

15
HOW ENTREPRENEURS ATTRACT GOOD LUCK

The more we know about what we really want, the better prepared we are to recognize favorable chances and extract good luck.

A.H.Z. Carr — *How to Attract Good Luck*

It's very common for authors of business and success books to insist that there's no such thing as luck. This is not true. There is, quite obviously, luck. People do "get discovered." Coincidences do turn to gain. For example, who I get sitting next to me in an airplane is the luck of the draw, yet, a number of times, conversations with those people have turned into business, opportunity, and income for me. Sure, I took the initiative to steer the conversation in productive directions, I was mentally prepared, and I was in the airplane, but, still, the luck of the draw put the right person beside me.

So, I believe in luck, I believe we get lucky breaks, and I don't think there's anything wrong with looking for a little luck and acknowledging it when we get it. On the other hand, let's remember that the lucky rabbit's foot sure didn't bring much luck to that rabbit.

Most entrepreneurs I deal with share a belief and cheerful expectation in luck, and try to do their part to facilitate it. They and I believe that an individual can learn to take certain actions that will, in effect, make him or her lucky.

USING YOUR SUBCONSCIOUS MIND

The biggest secret to deliberately making yourself lucky does not come as a set of concrete instructions — it has more to do with your subconscious mind. There just aren't enough pages in this book to convince you of the awesome power of your subconscious mind or how it works. I can only urge you to make a study of it on your own. You might want to begin with the excellent book, *Psycho-Cybernetics* by Dr. Maxwell Maltz.

I have thoroughly satisfied myself that the subconscious mind can be programmed or directed to search its vast stores to select, compile, and provide appropriate information and then give you the "flash of inspiration" you need to solve a nagging problem, go to the right place at the right time, say the right thing, or do the right thing. This is a computer-like function and most people can accept it as logical and true, even if they don't make a practice of using it. It's certainly nothing new; Thomas Edison used to lock himself in a quiet room, give commands to his subconscious mind, and, as he described it, "sit for ideas."

But the properly programmed and energized subconscious mind can go much further than that. Many very successful entrepreneurs, some scientists, and some psychologists believe that it can actually reach out and get needed information from the combined intelligence of the universe, and that it can set up a magnetic field that actually attracts the people, resources, and ideas needed to accomplish a particular goal.

The programming tool for unleashing the full powers of your subconscious mind is definition of purpose. The clearer your picture of what you want, the more activity you inspire inside your subconscious system. There are three main ways to put this to work and they all involve writing:

(a) *Continually develop your goals in writing.* Paul Meyer, founder of the Success Motivation Institute, says "If you are not making the progress you'd like to make, it is probably because your goals are not clearly defined." There is power in continually sharpening the definition of your goals on paper.

(b) *Write out your business plan.* A written, detailed business plan combines goal setting, action planning, and problem solving. It makes ideas believable.

(c) *Create and use daily checklists.* You wouldn't ever want to be on an airplane where the crew had reviewed the preflight processes by memory rather than by referring to checklists. Isn't your day and your use of your time equally important?

These three action steps have great practical value, but they also serve to communicate to your subconscious mind, in an organized manner, the seriousness of your objectives. Then wonderful things happen!

HOW TO BE IN THE RIGHT PLACE AT THE RIGHT TIME

Some years ago, I was navigating a troubled company through a turnaround and, fortunately, using all three of these action tools to the best of my ability. I put trust in my subconscious system (largely because there wasn't anything else around to trust) and, from time to time, got some very valuable "flashes."

For some time, I'd been thinking about the possibility of selling off part of the company's business in order to get new capital and strengthen the remaining business. One afternoon, a "flash" crystallized that for me; a plan came into my thoughts out of nowhere, to sell the manufacturing part of the company to a competitor in that arena, then use that capital to make the retail marketing part of the company stronger. It was all so clear in my mind that, that moment, I picked up the phone and called that competitor, got the president on the phone, and asked for an appointment to fly into his city and meet with him to discuss a business proposition. The next day, I described my proposal — with no preparation, just as it came to me — and immediately came to an agreement in principle. In just one week, the details were worked out, contracts signed, and an unprofitable part of my company's business was converted to a six-figure sum.

I later learned that I had selected the perfect time to approach this competitor. The president was right in the midst of deciding whether to more aggressively pursue additional business in the particular market in which we competed or to abandon that market and pursue expansion opportunities elsewhere. Had I been even a week later with my call, decisions would already have been made, possibly making our deal unworkable. Had I been a month or two earlier, the president would not have been ready. My timing was perfect. A lucky break?

No. Falling into deals like this is a result of having clearly defined goals, working hard, associating with people who could facilitate success, being involved in situations where opportunities can arise, and continuing personal education and improvement.

PERSISTENCE CAUSES LUCK, TOO

Last year, one of the direct-mail campaigns I put together brought in about $150,000 from a very small list in a matter of days. I was a hero. Observers commented on my remarkable good luck.

Nobody mentioned the dozen other campaigns I did that same month that got results ranging from mediocre to non-existent. I was involved in three very successful TV infomercials last year, too, totalling $80- to $100-million dollars in sales. But I was also involved in about 15 markedly unsuccessful ones.

To have good fortune, you have to do enough to help the pendulum swing in your direction. Quarterbacks that complete a lot of passes and throw a lot of touchdown passes throw a bunch of interceptions, too. Babe Ruth had more strikeouts than home runs. Edison had a warehouse full of failed, abandoned experiments. Just about every successful entrepreneur I know tries a lot of ideas every year and profits handsomely if only one or two succeed. One of my best clients tested six different "brilliant ideas" for doing more business with his past customers last year. Five of these ideas flopped. Each one was an embarrassment and a frustration. The sixth has turned into a million-dollar-a-year money machine.

LUCK IS A PRODUCT OF UNIVERSAL LAW

There are certain universal laws. Gravity, for example, works the same way every time, in every situation, for every one of us, whether we know about it or are ignorant of it, whether we think about it or not, whether we believe it or not. We accept that because we can prove it. Drop ten pencils, all ten fall to the ground.

Some other laws aren't so easily proven. My friend the late Foster Hibbard taught that the more you give, the more you get. I've found that the more you give, the more "luck" you get. I now use Hibbard's method for implementing this idea: you establish "the habit of giving" by opening up a separate, dedicated bank account, your "giving account." Into it you deposit from 1% to 10% of the money that comes to you from any and every source, and give that money away as you see fit, with no strings attached.

I'm here to tell you that giving away money this way is a fast path to wealth. It energizes the subconscious mind with a wealth and success consciousness unlike anything you've ever experienced.

I confess this was a very difficult idea for me to buy into. For one thing, it's illogical. If you have $2 and give away $1, you've got $1 left. You haven't increased your wealth, you've decreased it. Second, when I first started fooling around with this, I couldn't afford it. I didn't have any extra money. Third, you certainly can't call this businesslike. But I decided to test it, and I have now proven it works.

Let me say, though, that this works only when you strictly follow all the rules. You set up the account. You commit to a percentage. You put that percentage into your giving account every time you get money — no exceptions, no excuses. You give it away with no expectation of return. Try it for a couple of months and stay open to real serendipity and to new financial gain coming at you from the most unexpected sources.

SOME PRACTICAL ADVICE ON ATTRACTING GOOD LUCK

The simplest advice is to keep an open mind and gain a lot of exposure. You are sure to attract good luck this way. It's a big mistake to get myopic. Many businesspeople have tunnel vision and, as a result, they cut themselves off from opportunity altogether. Breakthrough ideas usually come from unusual sources, but if the clothing-store owner spends all day, every day in the store only stepping out to trade association meetings and conventions, he or she is letting luck come in through one very tiny hole. From businesspeople like this, you'll hear things like, "We've never done it that way before...That may be okay there, but not in our business." They close their minds and shut themselves off from the world.

Drive to your store or office by different routes. Every month, pick a magazine off the newsstand you've never read before and read it. Make a point of talking to cab drivers, restaurant servers, and others you might not normally strike up a conversation with. Give yourself little bits of exposure to ideas, experiences, and people outside the normal, narrow scope of your business and see what happens. Something will.

16
STAYING SANE IN AN INSANE WORLD

By night an atheist half believes in God.
Edward Young

The danger for the entrepreneur is to become totally absorbed in the success of the business to the detriment of all other parts of life. There are certainly times and circumstances when you must make your business your number-one priority, but there are also risks attached. But if you let your business become the only priority and become everything in your life, look out! Investing all your identity and self-esteem in a business takes away your opportunity to operate objectively and to change directions in your life as you learn, grow, and change.

HOW TO BE A BUSINESS SUCCESS AND HAVE IT NOT MATTER

In 1992, I was having my all-time, best-ever year in business. But one day I arrived home from a business trip to be told by my wife that she was leaving me. I feel very grateful that we have reconciled, but let me tell you, as the full impact of that evening set in, the fact that I was at the peak of success in my career became remarkably unimportant and unsatisfying.

Among other benefits, these events in my life led to the new idea that a person can have different, but equally important, priorities in life. You do not have to have a simple, vertical ladder with only one item on each rung. There are other ways to order the aspects of life. For me, business activities are fun and financial success is important, so business is a top priority. But my relationship with my wife has life-or-death importance to me too. My health is also important; without it, neither of the other two priorities can be given their due. So, rather than giving one of the three the top rung, I'm learning to give each a share of priority each and every day.

INTEGRITY IS IMPORTANT TOO

It is often easier to create temporary success if you ignore the issue of integrity. It may be tempting to rig product demonstrations, make false advertising claims, or cheat in other ways, but sooner or later, you're going to get caught — if not by the law, by unsatisfied customers.

Call it what you wish — karma, universal law, reciprocity, whatever — but what goes around does seem to come around. So the big question is, can you be a "nice guy" and a success in business too? Well, I don't know if I'd want to pit the late Mother Teresa against Donald Trump in a negotiation, but

129

that doesn't mean you have to operate without integrity to do well as an entrepreneur.

Integrity has become the hot marketing strategy of the 1990s. There are three basic categories of ethical standards in relationships between business and customers:

(a) *Minimum ethics.* We will do just enough to comply with all laws, stay out of jail, and deter lawsuits or returns for refunds.

Several years ago, at a seminar, on a dare, I made a list of ten well-known companies in diverse industries, all viewed as financially healthy at the time. I predicted they would be bankrupt within two years. My list was made up of businesses I believed were operating via this minimum standard. Two years later, seven of the ten were bankrupt and an eighth had been acquired while on the verge of bankruptcy. Just recently, one of the two remaining companies who beat my prediction announced first-quarter losses of $130 million and massive layoffs.

(b) *Average ethics.* We will give the customer fair exchange, reasonable value for their dollars, no less but no more. Most businesses operate at this stage. As a result, during good times, they'll get average results, turn a profit and stay in business.

(c) *Maximum ethics.* We will not ask how we can get more sales, we will ask how we can give more and better service. This is the right question.

The entrepreneur who constantly strives to be of greater and better service to his or her clientele has the edge in good times or bad. The entrepreneur constantly striving to better reward customers for their patronage is on ethical high ground and will be amply rewarded.

There are many good reasons for maximum ethical standards and behavior in business. Peace of mind is one of them.

Depending on spiritual beliefs, your seating assignment in the afterlife might be another. If no other reason motivates you, you might consider its value as plain, simple, good business.

For more about the place of ethics in business, see *Good Ethics, Good Business,* another title in the Self-Counsel Series.

HOW TO DEVELOP AND PROFIT FROM THE POWER OF FAITH

Reverend Robert Schuller often challenges people with the provocative question, "What plans would you have on your drawing board if you knew you could not fail?" Wouldn't it be wonderful to approach your daily activities with that kind of confidence. Well, you can. It is just an act of faith.

Personal faith is not usually a topic entrepreneurs discuss openly, but just about every highly successful person I've ever known has a very definite set of spiritual beliefs, and, as a result, acts with faith.

For me, faith is based on four simple ideas:

(a) There is plan and purpose behind our lives.

(b) We're here to learn some things and to accomplish some things.

(c) We were intended and are invited to live prosperously.

(d) When operating within certain parameters, we have every reason to expect positive results.

This solid expectation of positive results empowers you to cut through the clutter and confusion of self-doubt, fear, criticism, cynicism, negativism, and other obstacles.

For me, the parameters include the pursuit of goals that can be achieved by enriching others, not at the expense of others; accepting responsibility for my actions; and the pursuit of a purpose to which all goals relate. These are certainly not the only parameters for faith. Yours may very well differ from mine. It's not my purpose here to impose my spiritual beliefs on you or anybody else. But I feel that I would have presented an incomplete picture of what I've found necessary for entrepreneurial success without discussing this.

Lee Iacocca has written that you have to collect and evaluate accurate research data and other information in order to make good business decisions. He then says that, no matter how much information you get, it's never enough to guarantee the decision, and at some point you have to "take the leap of faith."

ENTREPRENEURS NEED EXTRAORDINARY FAITH IN THIS CRAZY WORLD

Is change more rapid and unpredictable than ever? It certainly seems that way. Globally, old enemies disappear or become new friends; old friends become new enemies. Who's who and what's what is uncertain and confusing. Governments are getting closer to having to pay the piper for mounting mammoth deficits, and nobody can be sure how that price will be extracted from our hides. In business, old industries die, new industries are invented; old reliable advertising methods fail, new strategies emerge. The rules change daily it seems. Competition is faster, smarter, tougher.

Ray Kroc made an interesting statement of faith in a TV interview some years ago when asked if he was ever irritated at how quickly his competitors copied everything McDonald's did. "Not at all," he replied. "We invent faster than they can copy."

That's what entrepreneurship is all about — confidently inventing new products, services, process, solutions. And the secret to sanity, even under intense pressure, even when confronted by confusing crisis, is to act with faith. It is that simple; take action.

Once, shortly after taking over a very troubled company, during a particularly difficult day, the corporation's

132

comptroller brought more bad news to my office: our most important, essential supplier had called and cut us off. Our company owed this vendor a large sum of money for past-due invoices and the vendor refused to ship the current order, which we needed desperately. There wasn't a dime in the checking account to give him.

What would you do?

I got on the first available plane to Minneapolis, and was parked on that vendor's doorstep when the president arrived the next morning. We sat down face to face and we worked out an agreement.

That "action model" has served me very well many times in my business career.

17

WHY AND HOW TO BUILD YOUR OWN MINICONGLOMERATE

It's an impossible situation,
but it has possibilities.

Sam Goldwyn

I'm often asked how I manage to keep up with all my different businesses. It puzzles many people. But one of the things they don't see is how my businesses and activities fit together, so that I view it as managing one conglomerate rather than wrestling with an assortment of different ventures.

Some of my companies share office and warehouse space, computer services, a telephone system, and some personnel. By sharing this way, each business entity gets better things than it could afford on its own, and no entity spends more than it has to for its needs. There's synergy at work, too. For example, one company produces videos and services a number of my consulting clients with infomercial and promotional video production. It also produces videos that my publishing company sells. My publishing company's catalogues also advertise my consulting, copywriting, and speaking services. My speaking activities provide new

134

customers for my publishing company's mailing lists. The books I write for other publishers, which are sold in bookstores, provide new customers for my company's mailing lists and provide consulting clients, so I count my writing as a form of advertising.

I have carefully and strategically started, acquired, and developed businesses and business interests that are profitable and valuable in and of themselves, but that also assist each other, so that the whole is greater than the parts. Many savvy entrepreneurs follow this same pattern.

Paul J. Meyer, founder of Success Motivation Institute (SMI) is one of the pioneering publishers and marketers of self-improvement and personal-growth self-study courses to individuals and corporate clients. SMI is a high-profile company, frequently advertising in business magazines such as *Success, Entrepreneur,* and *Inc.* Meyer is also a popular author and speaker, well-known for his works on goal-setting, sales skills, and business success. Most people see SMI as SMI, and that's it.

But Paul Meyer's great personal success and wealth has much more to do with his development of a miniconglomerate than with the SMI the public knows. For example, his conglomerate includes a vinyl package manufacturing company, which produces all the albums and cases for SMI's audiocassettes. His conglomerate includes one of the largest printing companies in the southwest United States, printing, of course, all of SMI's cassette labels, album covers, workbooks, books, brochures, and other materials. It also very effectively markets its printing capabilities to hundreds of outside client-companies. His conglomerate even includes real estate investment and property-management partnerships and companies that provide investment opportunities for his key executives.

On a bigger scale, consider the Disney empire. Its cable-TV Disney Channel is a business in and of itself, but also a huge promotional tool for its parks, movies, videos, and products. Its character-licensing business is immensely profitable, and everywhere those famous characters appear, they silently, subtly advertise other Disney products. Their mail-order business advertises their movies and parks and cross-promotes their retail stores. And on and on it goes.

This kind of "cross-fertilization," done carefully and intelligently, on a big or small scale, can make your business more profitable and a lot more fun. This is the way to milk a big income out of a small business.

Dan Kennedy's Eternal Truth #23
A "normal" small business can only yield a "normal" small-business income. To earn an extraordinary income, you must develop an extraordinary business!

STRENGTHEN YOUR CONGLOMERATE WITH STRATEGIC ALLIANCES

A long-time friend and business associate started a travel agency. The guarantee of my business alone made this an attractive business venture for him. For my allegiance, I got the convenience of instant, direct, unlimited access to the computer, the diligence of his staff, discounts, and some perks. But our alliance went further.

His travel agency and my speaking/seminar business shared the cost and use of an employee with computer skills. We shared a computer system. This resulted in my getting many of my mailing lists ship-shape at a bargain cost. For my $3,495-per-person direct-marketing conferences, his agency handled all the calls, airline and hotel reservations, and travel arrangements for my attendees and speakers. This arrangement provided my clients with an enhanced service and freed up my own staff from time-consuming responsibilities. It provided his agency with customers — and commissions — he'd never have got otherwise, with no marketing costs.

I created another alliance some years ago when my fledgling company lacked a solid credit standing and was having difficulty getting open credit with major vendors. A business friend of mine and I struck a bargain: I provided free consulting for some of his direct-mail projects and free use of my in-house recording studio for his occasional audio projects. In return, his more established company guaranteed an open credit line with the printing company I needed to do business with.

One of the tenants in our office building needed next-day and second-day letters and parcels packaged and shipped, but only two or three times a month. Since we had a shipping operation and staff, and they didn't, we arranged shipping for them. In exchange, we used their office copier, so we didn't have to buy, lease, rent, or maintain one.

These strategic alliances work to everyone's benefit. In the last example, we were easily able to accommodate the occasional shipping needs with our equipment and personnel, with no extra costs to our office. Without their copier, I would have paid $300 per month or more for a machine. That's $3,600 a year right to the bottom line. That's the equivalent of the gross profit on $9,000 to $10,000 worth of sales. Four or five similar, "little" strategic alliances can equate to $100,000 in business for my miniconglomerate! To me, that's real money.

HOW TO GET RICH BY ACCIDENT

The way to wealth as an entrepreneur is continually, creatively redefining and reinventing a business. Entrepreneurs need to be open to and alert for completely unexpected opportunities for alliances and ways to expand businesses on top of businesses. When you can do this, you can just about get rich by accident.

The large mail-order marketer of office supplies, Quill Corporation, provides a good example. They got in the mail-order business completely by accident. They originally had a tiny, struggling retail business, and to try and attract business, the owners experimented with sending out new product announcements and special offers on postcards. The response to their simple direct-mail campaigns was so good, they started selling directly rather than through the retail system.

The Miller brothers started Quill in 1957 in a remodeled coal bin in Chicago with $2,000 they managed to scrape together. Today, they mail over 45 million pieces a year, serve over 850,000 customers, generate nearly $350 million in sales, and work out of a 477,000-square-foot distribution center. "Being in the mail-order business was never our intention," Jack Miller says. "It just sort of happened."

In Phoenix, the "oldies" radio station, KOOL, won an award last year as the number-one "oldies" station in the country. But what interests me is their side business: a retail store that sells records of the 1950s and 1960s and memorabilia like Marilyn Monroe and Elvis collectibles, T-shirts, posters, and gifts. Evidently, the station managers kept getting calls and letters from people asking where they could find and buy particular records, so the company decided to open a retail store that provided the recordings the station played. Now the station promotes the store and the store promotes the station.

I also have an example from my own experience.

Item #1. In 1982, I was in my third year guest lecturing for a large-practice management firm in the chiropractic field. They charged their clients $30,000 each for a multi-year package of seminars and services. Just about every competitor in the field sold similarly expensive services, requiring big commitments.

Item #2. While speaking for this firm, I met another speaker with whom I was tremendously impressed. I believed then and still believe he is the very best motivational speaker ever. But I discovered, incredibly, that he wasn't working much.

Item #3. At the time, one of my businesses was a custom audiocassette manufacturing, packaging, and publishing company specializing in producing materials for professional speakers. I was stuck with the small, tight margins of a manufacturer and was urgently in need of increased revenue.

Then I put the pieces together. First, I detected an "opportunity gap." I figured if we went to these doctors with an offer of practice-building guidance priced a lot less than what was currently available, we'd have a unique opportunity to scoop up the majority who wanted help but wouldn't or couldn't commit to a high investment. So we built an audiocassette-based product around that idea, using this fantastic speaker, to be produced and controlled by my manufacturing company. Then we created a new seminar company and used direct mail to put 30 to 40 doctors in each free seminar, 4 or 5 nights a week in 4 or 5 different cities, where we sold the cassette-based system for $499.

From 1983 to 1985, this business venture sold over $1 million worth of merchandise. It provided a lot of work and an excellent income to the speaker, and it provided a lot of work for my manufacturing plant at much better-than-average profit margins. It even built a presence in that niche market and a mailing list that continues to generate profits today, purely via mail order. This million-dollar business was a happy accident.

Careful expansion and diversification, linking businesses within a business, forming strategic alliances, and keeping the doors wide open to accidental, additional opportunity, all added together can give the small-business entrepreneur a big income — a huge fortune.

18

USING YOUR BUSINESS AS A PATH TO FINANCIAL INDEPENDENCE

The only thing worse than not getting what you want is getting what you want.

Oscar Wilde

Why are you in business or getting into business?

You might be surprised at some of the answers I get when I ask this question of clients or at seminars. You see, getting into business is actually pretty easy, even too easy for some people's own good. Getting in is often a lot easier than getting out. And getting in is definitely a lot easier than getting what you really want from being in business. That's the tough assignment.

For starters, viewing your business as "the end" is a mistake. It's not an achieved goal; it is a means for achieving many other goals. For too many people, the desire to own their own business is so powerful and exciting that little thought is given to "what's next?"

You don't want to marry the business. Marry the goals.

Margie N.'s experience provides a great example. Margie N. determined that she wanted to open her own muffin and cookie store. She researched the field, found a location she believed was viable, and developed some of her own creative recipes. She was very excited about her business plan. At night, she lay awake, staring at the ceiling, visualizing her sign — Margie's Famous Muffins & Munchies — over the door of her store.

After some struggle to get the money together, Margie opened her shop just as she had visualized it. Just one month later, she was in financial trouble. The location wasn't as "hot" as she'd believed, and there were other problems. But, by happy accident, the manager of a near-by warehouse store stopped in and was so impressed with Margie's muffins that he asked her to supply her products for resale in his store. That was a big success, quickly requiring a full night-shift operation to meet the demand.

The retail store was losing money, but the wholesale baking operation was a success. Finally, Margie did the obvious and closed down the high-rent, unsuccessful retail location and put the wholesale baking operation in a cheap rental space. But she cried for a week over the death of her dream. By the end of that year, she was supplying three of the warehouse stores plus numerous restaurants and made a huge net profit. She's got the makings of an enormously successful business, but not the business she originally mentally married, and that caused her quite a bit of emotional distress.

When I talked with her at length about all this, I redirected her toward a variety of interesting, exciting goals, including remodeling her house, traveling, writing a book, establishing an investment program with a $500,000 value target in ten years, and more. Now, not having to be at her retail business every day and with the financial freedom from the high rent, she has the opportunity to expand by selling new accounts.

DON'T LET YOUR BUSINESS OWN YOU

It's ironic that in order to get what you really want from owning your own company — wealth, security, freedom, for example — you must do the most unnatural, difficult thing for an entrepreneur; you must systematically reduce the dependency of the business on you. Don't overlook this. This is *the* secret to becoming financially independent through entrepreneurship.

Most entrepreneurs have no understanding of this and give it very little thought until it's too late. They wind up being owned by their businesses. To their surprise, they find that they've traded one old boss for a plethora of new ones: stockholders, investors and lenders, employees and associates, customers and clients, vendors and government agencies. Their ideas of independence dissolve against these forces.

There's an old joke about the government bureaucrat descending on the small-business owner. He says: "We've received a report that you have some poor fellow working here 18 hours a day, 7 days a week, for nothing but room, board, meals, all the tobacco he can smoke and all the liquor he can drink. Is that true?" "Yes, I'm afraid it is," admits the owner. "And I'm sad to say, you're looking at him."

You're probably wondering about the security of your business. If the typical entrepreneur leaves the business alone for a week, it does a Jekyll-and-Hyde transformation. You have got to be there! I know many business owners who go years without a vacation. And, those who do go on vacation don't enjoy. One half hopes everything's okay back at the ranch, which he or she checks every few hours by phone, and the other half is disappointed if it is okay; after all, how could it be without his or her indispensable presence?

Too many people get into business only to discover they've acquired a new, tougher, more demanding, more stressful job, and they cannot see any way to change it.

The trick is to let the business mature — and the faster, the better. An immature business is entrepreneur driven. In its early days, that's okay and usually necessary. You are the business. From day one, though, if your business is to provide security, freedom, and wealth, you should be working at weaning the business from dependence on you and creating dependence on systems.

GETTING OUT OF YOUR OWN WAY

Some people tie their egos up in their minute-by-minute, indispensable importance to their businesses. I have made this mistake myself: carrying data around in my head, making every decision myself whether for a dime or a dollar, being the first one at the office in the morning, the last one there at the end of the day, the guy with the beeper and a cellular phone, able to do every job in the place — and meddling in every one of them.

I was probably indispensable and irreplaceable. I was also stressed out — a nervous breakdown looking for a place to happen. I started getting in the habit of stopping off "for a couple of drinks" after leaving the office and going home hours later, half-drunk. This is not the way to get your sense of importance satisfied.

Instead, you can be important and make the most meaningful contributions to your business — without sacrificing your health, family and sanity — by freeing yourself from in-depth involvement in day-to-day operations, so you have more time for the few creative things you do best. In my case, in my publishing company, what I do best is create new products or improve the ones we already have, create advertising and marketing materials, and deal with key clients and contacts. But if I give equal time to purchasing raw materials

143

and supplies, bookkeeping, organizing records and mailing lists, product quality control, and so on, I cheat the business out of my best and I cheat myself out of the business's best.

Be sure you're not cheating yourself and your business out of your best.

HOW TO HELP YOUR BUSINESS MATURE

A mature business is some or all of these things:

- MARKET driven
- PRODUCT driven
- SERVICE driven
- SYSTEMS driven

For example, a retail store in a busy mall is driven by its market. Very little, if any, outside advertising or marketing is done; the business is designed to feed off the mall traffic. A manufacturer of a little widget that goes inside a bigger widget that makes the windshield wiper switch work is product driven. The bigger widget maker has to have the little widget; the little widget is only made by a couple of companies. A quick-copy shop is service driven; its customers are usually concerned with and wooed by speed, convenience, and reliability.

In the beginning, these businesses will also be owner driven. The retail-store owner makes all the product, pricing, sales, window-display, and other decisions for the store. The manufacturer watches over the widget making, hiring, firing, buying raw materials, keeping the customers happy, and so on. The copy-shop owner solicits accounts, deals with customers, and keeps the copy shop hopping.

Over time, these businesses can mature to a great degree. Each owner can isolate the one or two things he or she does best and delegate the rest. But the way to get to that stage is to develop your systems, and the development of effective *marketing* systems is the most vital job overlooked by most entrepreneurs.

For example, consider John G., a roofing contractor. He told me that he wanted to diminish his day-to-day work in the business, but as he is the one who brings in most of the business, he doesn't know how to go about it. He's been able to hire good crews and good managers and delegate all the labor, but, he asked, how do you delegate the prospecting and selling that gets the jobs?

The answer is to develop a marketing system that delivers predictable results from repetitive use. In John's case, we worked together to create a direct-mail campaign aimed at qualified leads (provided by a list broker), then a telephone procedure to convert a predictable number of those inquiries to appointments. Then, the big step, we worked on a standardized sales presentation using a flip chart, a video, and a cost-quoting computer program. This made it possible to hire sales representatives, train them quickly and easily, and put them in the field to secure just about the same number of jobs per appointments as when John dealt personally with all the customers. Bingo! This fellow was able to replace himself with a marketing system.

Over the next two years, not only did John achieve his objective of cutting by half the time devoted to the business, but the business was able to increase by nearly 30%!

Dan Kennedy's Eternal Truth #24
Passion wanes with longevity
and familiarity.

The time to start thinking about all this is not 6 or 12 months before you'd like to change your role in your business. In fact, you should start planning for flexibility and change from day one. You must accept that the unbridled passion you

145

feel for your business at the beginning, that has you happily there from dawn to midnight up to your armpits in work, *will* change as time passes. The activity you can't wait to get at today may bore the blazes out of you three years from now. It's smart to build your business in a way that allows you to satisfy your changing interests.

You can also think of this as a form of insurance. Life is uncertain — eat dessert first! You could be injured or become ill. Who knows? The statistics I've seen indicate that one of every three business owners experience some period of disability during their careers. For many, even with an insurance policy in their desk drawer, this can kill the business. Imagine, though, how much more likely it will be that your business can survive a period of months without you if you've structured it with systems from the very beginning.

The first thing you must do is ensure that the routine processes of your business are really routine. That means they happen by procedure so that just about anybody can step in and follow those procedures. You shouldn't have to have your nose in everything.

Second, you need to develop your business to the point where new customers or clients are attracted to your company by marketing systems, not through your direct personal efforts.

Third, you must have a plan for directing more and more of your time and energy to the few aspects of the business you enjoy and do best and for reducing the commitment of your time and energy to the many aspects of the business you do not enjoy or do best.

HOW DOES A SYSTEM WORK?

First and foremost, a system works without you being married to it 24 hours a day. Let's say that there have been a number of burglaries in your neighborhood, and you're suddenly more concerned than usual with making your home looked occupied all the time. One way to do that is to stay home. Another would be to hire a house-sitter for the times you aren't there — in other words, delegating the responsibility. Or, you could get some simple, inexpensive electronic devices that can be set to turn different lights and appliances on and off at different times. That would be a system. Once in place, it works with little or no attention from you.

Systems deliver predictable and consistent results.

A marketing system is arguably the most important kind of system that an entrepreneur can ever give the business. One restaurant owner I know, Bill H. exemplifies the success of initiating such a system. He sends two letters and a postcard to residents of the neighborhoods surrounding his restaurant and to people in businesses around his restaurant. He has this system streamlined to the point that he has a formula for determining what percentage of responses he will get from each mailing, and how many of those responses turn into reservations and revenue for his restaurant. This means he can guarantee his restaurant a certain predictable base of business each and every week. If, say, a seasonal slump is coming up, he can increase the number of letters mailed in order to increase revenue. He can go to sleep at night knowing that a certain number of new customers will call the next day, and, because this is an entirely mechanical process, he could go on vacation for three weeks and still guarantee a certain amount of business to his restaurant. His system gives him immense power, leverage of time, less stress and frustration, and better positioning with new clients.

Always strive to put systems in place; the right systems can totally transform a business.

Note: A free report, "How to Create Marketing Systems for Any Business" is available on request from the author, c/o Kennedy & Associates, 5818 N. 7th Street #103, Phoenix, Arizona 85014.

19
HOW TO GET A BUSINESS OUT OF TROUBLE

*One ought never to turn one's back on a
threatened danger and try to run away
from it. If you do that, you will double the
danger. But if you meet it promptly and
without flinching, you will reduce it by half.
Never run away from anything. Never.*

Winston Churchill

Maybe you'll never need the advice in this chapter. Maybe.

I have been involved in a couple of business turnarounds
and helped clients with others. I've also made a point of
studying some of the best-known, big-name turnaround experts, and I can tell you that there is very little difference
between getting one business or another out of trouble. Your
options for action are rather limited.

The very first, crucial step is honesty. You've got to forget
all about protecting your ego and blaming others. None of
that matters when the kettle is boiling over. You have to
diagnose and identify problems, period. You need all the gory
details. No one can be allowed to hide anything; no one can
be allowed to feel they have to hide anything.

This is very tough to achieve. Everybody's natural responses are to cover their own tracks as best they can. If people can't or won't be honest with themselves and each other about the problems, either the people have to go, fast, or the business goes under. That's it.

AS LONG AS THERE'S A PULSE, THERE'S HOPE

The only absolutely certain death blow for a troubled business is running out of cash. There's little else that's irreversible.

Poisoned Tylenol killed people but the business survived. Auto makers routinely recall thousands of cars with potentially lethal defects but they survive. Key people quit, big competitors move in, fires and floods happen, but businesses survive. I don't think there's any business problem that can't be beat as long as there's cash flow. During a turnaround period, profit and loss is even irrelevant. But cash flow is everything.

I've run a company completely out of cash on two occasions. Miraculously, this company got through both these situations. On one of those occasions, the company took five weeks to recover from a $47,000 checking account overdraft. I spent those five weeks walking around with just a few crinkled dollar bills in my pocket, coasting downhill in my car to conserve gas, jumping out of my skin at every phone call, just waiting for the final death nudge to come from somewhere. I've faced cash-flow problems since, but I learned my lesson. No matter the pressure, I will not take a business down to zero cash.

If you find your business in a cash-flow crunch, you must immediately become very tight-fisted about parting with each penny. Pay bills in tiny pieces. Trickle it out. Negotiate new terms with vendors as fast as you can. Sacrifice some vendors if you must. Put tiny dabs of grease on the squeakiest wheels. But never, never spend down to zero or, worse, below zero, to appease the wolves. Let them stand out there baying and scratching at the door, but keep a few spare bullets in your gun at all times.

FORGET "KINDER AND GENTLER"

Cut costs with an axe, not a surgical knife. If there's any turnaround mistake I've made more than once, it's being too gentle and conservative in the cutting. You can always put a person or function back in if you must. To start getting out of trouble, though, swing your axe in a wide arc. Cut everywhere. Spare no one, no thing. Cut, cut, cut.

In one turnaround situation, I let 38 people go in one day. I had more blood on my hands than the monster in a cheap horror movie. It was really awful. One of the top people asked me: "How do you know you can function without some of these people?" I said: "I don't." I really didn't. I didn't have time to sort out who was really important and who wasn't. I had to stop the cash hemorrhage first, to even get a minute to think. So I swung the axe with abandon. And I'd do it again without a second thought if presented with a similar situation.

PULL TOGETHER A PLAN

Once you've done what you can to stop the cash from pouring out of the business's wounds, bring everything to a near stop for a few days, get the best brains together you can, lock yourselves up in a quiet room without interruptions, and pull together a plan.

Without a plan, you'll make the mistake I made in the first turnaround crisis I dealt with. I started out by instantly reacting to each and every new problem that reared its ugly head, each howling wolf as it appeared at the door. I'd drop one thing to face the other, then turn from that to the next noise in the dark. Pretty soon I was spinning around like a top. One night, long after everybody else had left, I was in my chair behind my desk, sweaty, bone tired, exhausted. I realized I was completely out of control.

150

Then I shut the door and put together a believable, step-by-step business plan with a lot of detail for the first six months and more general ideas for the next six. With this battle plan in hand, I had confidence, I had the ability to engineer cooperation and trust from others. Then I placed a limit on the amount of time each day dedicated to problems. When we hit the quota for the day, that was it; the rest of the problems had to stand in line until the next day. Each day, I set aside a certain amount of time to implement the business plan. With plan in hand, I restored order and kept myself out of the padded room.

DON'T HIDE

If your business owes a lot of money to a lot of creditors, you'll be tempted to hide. Big mistake. You or someone you give this responsibility to must keep the lines of communication open for those creditors and be as truthful as possible with them. When you can't promise a payment amount and date, don't; promise what you can — a date and time you'll next communicate.

Target the creditors hurting your cash flow most for comprehensive renegotiation. Take your new business plan and meet in person if possible. At the least, phone or fax them, and shoot for the very best deal you can get.

For example, let's say you owe XYZ Company $20,000, all past due. You might get that $20,000 switched from a trade payable to a long-term, five-year installment note, interest only for the first year, and agree on new purchases to pay one-third with order, one-third on delivery, and one-third in

30 days. This takes $20,000 out of your current struggle altogether. Otherwise, you'd be nicking away at that $500 or $1,000 at a time, the creditor would never be happy, and getting needed goods would probably be next to impossible.

Facing trouble head-on, more often than not, earns respect and promotes cooperation.

DON'T TAKE IT PERSONALLY

Okay, your business is in trouble and you were captain of the ship while it smashed into the rocks. That's bad. But everybody makes mistakes. You're not the first, you won't be the last, and there is no shame in screwing up. The only cause for shame would be giving up without a fight. If you are genuinely trying to do the best you can, there's nothing to be ashamed of.

Beating yourself up or letting somebody else beat you up as a person is uncalled for and, obviously, unproductive. You have to be able to step out of the emotion and be a tough-minded turnaround consultant for your own business.

GET HELP

Depending on the size and type of your business, there will also be legitimate, qualified experts available as consultants to help you in the turnaround. At the very least, if you haven't already formed and frequently sought advice from your own "master-mind group," now is the time to do it. You may consider seeking free consulting assistance from SCORE (the Service Corps of Retired Executives, accessible through your local SBA office) in the United States or from the Business Development Bank of Canada (BDC).

Don't rely only on yourself during troubled times. Everybody can use a boost at one time or another. Seeking help at the right time from the right sources is a sign of strength, not a sign of weakness. That's a lot easier to write down on paper than to accept, but it is true.

DIRECT YOUR ENERGY TO BUSINESS RENOVATION

Even if it's only an hour, grab a certain amount of time each and every day and go to work on reinventing your business. Get to the very core of the problems. During a turnaround, you'll be doing a lot of patching work, and that's okay, but while you're patching up cuts and bruises you need to be the visionary designer of a whole new and improved operation.

Don G. had a chain of six restaurants that wound up in deep trouble. While he did all the things we've been talking about with the entire chain, he also took just one of the locations as his "new" model, and made major changes there, literally inventing a new and different restaurant operation, from A to Z. After a year, the entire company had limped its way back into positive cash flow, largely through debt restructuring and cost cutting, and although the whole business was still operating at a net loss, the new model was consistently hitting the 30% profit mark. Don now had a model to duplicate in his other five locations, which allowed him to again restructure debt, get some new investment capital, quickly make over the other five locations, and by the end of the second year of the turnaround, chalk up several hundred thousand dollars in profit.

At this point, the local beer distributor who supplied his restaurants bought into his company, contributed enough capital to wipe out all the high-interest debt, and open four more locations. Three years later, they sold the entire business to a national food-service company and walked away millionaires.

If Don had waited until he had his entire turnaround process implemented to go to work on his core business's reinvention, all these good things would not have happened, and he might have run out of time and money before ever getting to try his new plan.

20
HOW TO KEEP YOUR BUSINESS FROM GETTING YOU INTO TROUBLE

If you don't know where you're going,
any road will take you there.

The Cheshire Cat in *Alice In Wonderland*

Here's a surprisingly soft-hearted chapter to end an otherwise pretty hardheaded book. And here's advice that's much easier to give than to live. Nevertheless, to omit this, which would have been easy, would be to leave you with a misleading view of my beliefs about *total* entrepreneurial success.

With just about every business I've started, I've immersed myself in 18-hour days, dozing on my desk. And you will too. But — and this is a very big but — if you permit this to extend itself, to become a way of life, please hear this warning: you're headed for a big crash.

I've gradually learned that when you push too hard and too long without letting up, you become less and less effective, it takes more and more effort to push the pea up the hill, and you wind up trapped in a very vicious cycle: ever-increasing strain required for ever-decreasing results. But all that's minor compared to the likely big crashes.

154

BIG CRASH #1: "GOOD-BYE"

I told you earlier in this book that, in 1992, my marriage came apart. If you really love your spouse, as I did and do, nothing quite compares with having him or her look you square in the eye and say "I don't love you anymore. Good-bye." After the initial shock, dismay, anger, resentment, fear, etc. had passed, I came to the conclusion that nothing I'd been doing or was doing in my businesses mattered much without her in my life.

I am not going to belabor my personal experience here. However, if you are in a relationship that really matters to you, don't risk any assumptions about how understanding that other person is going to be. Instead, ask yourself whether you're willing to permanently sacrifice that person and that relationship for your business. If not, you cannot neglect the relationship, even for a day.

Also, being actively in love happens to be healthy and good for you. Giving some time and energy — both emotional and physical — to your mate every day will enhance, not detract from your entrepreneurial performance. I know that's hard to believe when mired in the pressures of getting a business going, but trust my experience here — it's true.

BIG CRASH #2: "MY HEART ATTACKED ME"

Entrepreneurs who completely sacrifice their health for "the cause" are common. And, of course, I've made that mistake too — although I'm taking corrective actions while still relatively young and still, fortunately, in generally good health. So with the grace of God, a little luck, and the discipline to keep going with a health and longevity program, I'll avoid this big crash.

I'm a long way away from being a health expert. But I've seen enough friends and business acquaintances hit this wall to make some observations about the most certain causes of the crash: immersion in extended periods of stress and pressure without relief, a general lack of stress management skills, a lousy diet, carrying too much weight, drinking too much booze and coffee, smoking, and getting too little sleep and no exercise.

Some years back, during a difficult time in my business, I lapsed into the habit of hitting the cocktail lounge every evening, after 14-hour days, drinking my dinner, getting home by auto-pilot, and tossing and turning all night while my system struggled to work off the alcohol. I jump-started myself each morning with pots of coffee and sugar doughnuts, and then started doing it all over again. This way of life didn't solve any problems, and it's a wonder I didn't pay a big, big price, like a drunk-driving arrest or, worse, an accident, a divorce, or some kind of physical collapse.

I'm not advocating that you become militant in your exercise or diet routines, but, on the other hand, I'd bet you could stand to take better care of yourself. If you had a $100,000 racehorse, would you keep it up all night smoking and drinking, give it coffee and doughnuts in the morning, only exercise it once a month, and feed it at McDonald's every day? I'd bet you'd protect your investment a little more carefully than that. So, let's be smart about this. The most important piece of equipment, the most valuable asset, the thing most in need of protection in your business is you.

WHY PUT IT OFF UNTIL TOMORROW WHEN YOU CAN STALL UNTIL NEXT WEEK?

I know. You're too busy to think about this stuff now. You need to make some money. Get your business to a certain point, then you'll re-energize your romance, then you'll go on a diet. Then.

People install fire alarms after fires, burglar alarms after robberies, get self-defense training after a mugging, and on and on. If you could buy life insurance after you died, that industry would be 1,000 times bigger. You know that "point" you're going to reach in your business when you're going to attend to these other things? That "point" keeps moving.

156

There will always be another point to get to. In the meantime, you and your spouse grow apart, your kids grow up, and your stomach gets bigger.

If you're going to put something off, put off a business meeting, a phone call, an ad deadline, or a presentation. Take it off today's page and deliberately put it on tomorrow's. Surprisingly, most business things will keep for a few days. I've learned this the hard way. It was in my nature to get everything done today. The problem with trying to get everything down now is that quality suffers. I've come to the conclusion that most entrepreneurs will become twice as successful by cutting their "haste" by half.

QUALITY, NOT QUANTITY

You've heard the "work smarter, not harder" adage. It's valid. To succeed as an entrepreneur, you have to learn how to get maximum value from small chunks of time. Working hard, long hours is not the secret to entrepreneurial success. If you've been raised with the "hard work ethic" this is going to seem strange to you, but the secret is time brilliantly invested in high-pay-off activity, not just time invested. When you understand this, you can also take a different, more sensible approach to living life every day. There *is* time to exercise. There *is* time to take an evening walk. There *is* time to go to the mall and find a gift for your mate. There *is* time to sit down and watch a TV program without a pile of paperwork in your lap.

Right now, as I write this book, I'm making some significant changes in one of my businesses, so significant it's like reinventing it. So, here I am, in the throes of entrepreneurial start-up again. But this time, I'm doing it without turning out the lights on life. I'm taking time out for a little exercise (almost) every day, for my weekly massage, to make a glass of juice with my juicer, to have dinner with my wife, and to go to lunch with a friend. And, surprise! I'm finding my work time more effective and productive than ever, my mind clearer, my energy better. I'm trading quantity for quality.

If you were my very best friend, I'd tell you to really think about what is in this chapter. Don't just say to yourself, well, that's nice, and then go on as always. Don't let your business get you into trouble.

21
A NO B.S. REPORT ON THE INTERNET AND OTHER TECHNOLOGY

"You know you've lost control of your computer when the mouse orders from the International House of Cheese's Web site on the Internet."

Dr. Herb True

Since this book was first published in 1993, the world has seen a huge surge in the types and quality of technology available to average citizens. As I was preparing this latest edition, my publisher asked me to both update the existing book and add my comments on the very topical and timely subject of today's high technology and how it pertains to business success. In this new chapter, I will discuss the Internet, broadcast fax, fax-on-demand, voice mail, and audio and video brochures.

I can tell you from working with the thousands of business people who subscribe to my newsletter that there is tremendous interest in using leading edge technology for marketing and money-making purposes, and the Internet heads up that list. Apparently, all the hype, talk, and publicity about the Internet has really stimulated a lot of folks.

Regrettably, I'm here mostly to rain on all that excitement. In my view, making money via the Internet is grossly over-hyped. Here are some of the claims:

(a) Millions and millions of people are flooding onto the Net, running around looking at Web sites, and buying everything that isn't nailed down.

(b) If you don't have your own Web site and e-mail address, you're as out of touch as somebody still writing letters with a manual typewriter or washing clothes on a rock in the river.

(c) The gold rush is now. The longer you wait, the more expensive and difficult it will be to get involved.

(d) Using the Internet is like getting free advertising — how can you say no to that?

Now I'd like to give you my no B.S. take on these claims, and I want to qualify it a bit. First, I'll confess I'm far from a techie. I use my computer as a typewriter and I don't like it very much. So there's no doubt I come to discussions of technology with a bias.

I should also mention that I am on a friendly basis with several of the most highly respected experts in the Internet field. One of my biggest clients, the Guthy-Renker Corporation, has a division known as Guthy-Renker Internet that operates one of the largest, if not the largest, Internet mall — America's Choice Mall. In addition, in 1996 and 1997, I directed an exhaustive analysis of marketing through the Internet for a client, including reviews of literally every book, report, course, and seminar on the subject. I do have a Web site myself at: www.inner-circle.com, although, quite frankly, it has proven to be of nominal value.

With skepticism high but hope intact, I continually look at everything all my clients, subscribers, and researchers can find, produce, or suggest with regard to making money via the Internet.

With all that said, here are some of the hard, cold realities about this fascinating, exciting but largely disappointing media.

KNOCK, KNOCK, WHO'S THERE?

Let's start with the millions of people who are on-line, using the Internet. The truth is that nobody, and I mean nobody, knows what the real number of users is. When you see a company like America Online or CompuServe talk about the huge number of new subscribers to their service each month, you need to know the number of drop-outs, too. As near as I can tell, in any given time period, they lose about as many as they gain.

What's probably more important is the size of the Internet economy. Here, for example, are the rough numbers: in 1996, people bought about $75 billion worth of merchandise from mail-order catalogues compared with $200 million to $1 billion of purchases directly via the Internet. That should give you an idea of the relative importance of the business done via the Internet — it may be as much as 1/75th the size of the traditional mail-order industry. Probably even less. Or, look at it this way: all the commerce conducted on the Internet equals the total business of just one or two big mail-order companies.

By the way, the most reliable studies I've seen indicate that only 4% to 5% of the entire U.S. population is on-line. But if you subtract from that the number of primary users under the age of 16, the number of students, government agencies, and others using it only for research, and the vast majority of business people using it only for e-mail, who do you have left? My research says less than 2% of the population might be potential customers for your products and services. And keep in mind you'll be competing for their attention with tens of thousands of other Web sites in a disorganized, chaotic environment.

The difficulty of using the Internet and the clogging of the Internet prompted an article in the January 1996 issue of Popular Mechanics magazine entitled, "Death of the Internet." America Online's much publicized problems, including the class action lawsuit by its subscribers, are a microcosm of the entire Internet world. People frequently encounter busy signals and long waits for access through their service providers, difficulty finding what they want once connected, poorly designed Web sites that take forever to access, and eventually, disappointment with the whole thing.

WHAT ARE INTERNET USERS REALLY BUYING?

One of the many obstacles to making money on the Internet is that those things that cyberspace browsers are really interested in may not match up with what you have to sell. While it is difficult to get any reliable numbers, a compilation of experts' educated guesses indicates that 30% to 60% of all commerce on the Internet has to do with one thing and one thing only — sex.

Even the staid Wall Street Journal has run a front page article reporting on the millions of dollars being made with sex-related goods and services on the Internet. Their article featured a former strip club dancer named Danni Ashe and her success on the Internet selling adult videos, magazines, autographed pictures, used underwear, and access to chat rooms and interactive activities. And she is not alone, many other businesses has even more exhaustively covered this same subject. Virtually everybody who was and is selling sex-related entertainment via magazines and 900 telephone numbers has rushed to the Internet. Their extraordinary prosperity tells you a lot about the average cyberspace customer and just what that customer is interested in buying.

Here is the data from a sample month in 1997: Yahoo!, the number one search engine on the Internet published a ranking of the top 200 search word requests. Sixty percent of the top twenty and 25% of all of them are sex-related. Seven of the top ten are sex oriented. Here's the top twenty with traffic counts, in order:

1.   Sex 1,553,420
2.   Chat 414,320
3.   XXX 397,640
4.   Playboy 390,920
5.   Netscape 350,320
6.   Nude 292,560
7.   Porno 257,860
8.   Games 217,440
9.   Porn 199,180
10. Weather 190,900
11. Penthouse 186,840
12. Pamela Anderson 172,760
13. Pornography 172,260
14. P**** 169,840
15. Persian kitty 163,620
16. Maps 163,360
17. Halloween 155,680
18. Music 151,780
19. Adult 148,960
20. Chat rooms 139,960

And here are a few selected sites, to give you even more of a picture of how the Internet is dominated (pardon the pun) by sexual content:

50. Tits 74,080
64. Lesbians 64,24

90.	Free sex 54,240
97.	Babes 52,220
112.	Nude pictures 47,460
119.	Naked 46,840
123.	Cyberporn 45,320
127.	Oral sex 44,820
177.	Spanking 37,180

Doesn't this all resemble the kids' game of looking up dirty words in the dictionary? Unfortunately, it reflects the current culture of the Internet and tells you what the browsers are really looking for. In fact, sex has become such a big part of Internet commerce, the opportunity to participate in profits from adult Web sites is regularly advertised in the business opportunity classifieds of USA Today and marketed to investors through other media. One of the biggest corporations in the adult publishing business even advertises its own public stock offering on the same Web site where its adult videos, product catalogues, and interactive sex clinic are advertised (intimatetreasures.com).

CONSUMERS STILL FEAR THE INTERNET

Another barrier to commerce on the Internet is the reality and public perceptions about the security of credit card transactions. According to one survey of confirmed Internet users published in Dartnell Corporation's Sales & Marketing Report, 94% are not comfortable releasing financial information over the Internet to firms they have not previously done business with, 41% immediately exit Web sites when asked for information about themselves, and 27% register with false information. Another study published in the October 1997 issue of the Internet Marketing and Technology Report shows that a whopping 78% of Web site visitors refuse to provide information when visiting a site. This raises the question: if you can't find out any information about prospective customers who visit your site, what good is the site?

In reality, both security for credit card transactions and general privacy protection is continually improving on the Internet, but it is still a far cry from safe. And most people still distrust Internet commercial transactions.

Yet another barrier is that buying via the Internet requires customers to totally alter ingrained shopping behavior. In an article in *Inc. Technology*, Glenda Shasho Jones, a direct-mail consultant, noted that shopping at a real mall is a physical and social activity, and you get to touch, feel, even try on merchandise, as well as talk with sales clerks and meet friends for lunch. In contrast, shopping at home with a catalogue is what she calls a desultory activity; something to do while you are doing something else, such as watching TV. Shopping via the Internet requires you to stare at the screen and give it your attention, so it's almost as physically demanding as going to the mall, but without the benefits. It's not analogous to catalogue or in-person shopping. It is a totally new behavior.

Presumably it is the combination of all these barriers that keeps real, diversified commerce from developing on the Internet. The categories where you can find any significant success stories are few. As I noted, sex is one. Computer-related products and services is, naturally, another. For example, a business called MacOutlet run by a 13-year-old kid reportedly sold over $800,000 worth of computer products last year entirely through a combination of its Web site, e-mail, fax, and phone. Another successful category is gambling-related businesses.

Generally, the success stories seem to be fairly isolated. Amazon Books is a Web site everybody talks about, although it remains to be seen if it can survive recent on-line competition from both Barnes & Noble and Wal-Mart. Virtual Vineyards is another, often-presented success. I find that everybody who hypes the Internet talks about this same handful of examples.

Earlier this year, I used my newsletter, which reaches thousands of business people each month, to invite anybody with tax records and other documentation indicating success selling something other than sex, gambling, computer products or psychics on the Internet to step forward. I even offered a financial reward. Only one person did. And she was marketing services to computer consultants.

BE THERE OR BE SQUARE

Now let's tackle the second idea that if you don't have your own Web site and e-mail address on your business card, everybody will think you're some kind of dinosaur, hopelessly out of touch. Unless you are in a technology-oriented business, this simply isn't true. For example, one recent survey of Fortune 1000 CEOs indicated that fewer than 5% of these executives had ever used e-mail. Over the past few months, I've surveyed about 3,000 small business owners and sales professionals and found about 10% using e-mail, hardly any going to Web sites to find or buy products and services. I wasn't, therefore, surprised to read a *Wall Street Journal* article reporting that fewer than 1% of small business owners who own computers use the Internet.

This doesn't mean you shouldn't use e-mail or even have your own Web site, but you certainly shouldn't let yourself be stampeded into it. The Internet is full of Web sites put up by businesspeople pressured into doing so that are badly designed, unproductive, and now neglected. Huge sums of money are wasted by people feeling forced or hurried to get on the Internet just because their competitors are there or because they're hearing so much about it. My favorite western philosopher, Texas Bix Bender, author of the book *Don't Squat With Yer Spurs On*, observes that "just 'cause you're following a well-marked trail don't mean that whoever made it knew where they were goin'."

There are ways to utilize e-mail or offer e-mail communication to those who wish to reach you that way without going on-line yourself. ATG Technologies offers a service where they'll receive e-mail for you, translate it, and send it to you by voice mail or fax. You can then dictate a reply to their computer over the phone and ATG will translate your reply into outgoing e-mail.

By the way, it's very unlikely to get more expensive to get involved with the Internet in the future. In fact, the opposite is going to be true, just as it has been with all technology. Today's fax machines cost 1/5th as much as the early models did. I remember paying $299 for my first hand-held calculator. Today you can buy a better one for $9.95. In the beginning, it was common to pay thousands of dollars to have a Web site designed; now the cost is under $1,000 in most cases, and there's even off-the-shelf software that lets you do it yourself.

BUT THE GOLD RUSH IS ON AND YOU DON'T WANT TO BE LAST, DO YOU?

How about the gold rush idea? The promoters of Web sites and Internet malls love using this analogy; that this is like the great gold rush and those who get there first will get the gold. Another analogy they love is the real estate comparison; get a prime site in this mall or that mall now, before the price skyrockets. These analogies are ridiculous because unlike gold mines and locations in physical malls, there is an unlimited amount of Internet space. People can make as many Web sites as they want and an Internet mall doesn't actually have any prime sites. Will Rogers advised: "Buy real estate because they ain't making more of it." Well, they ARE making more real estate on the Internet — lots of it.

Some say that the people who sold the shovels to the gold miners made more money than most miners did. So far, that is definitely true of the Internet. The people selling Web sites, mall sites, and services are making a lot more money than the Internet merchants buying them.

One of the earliest developments of Internet malls, Cyber-mall Corporation, closed in 1997, cutting loose about 70 clients with about 1,200 Web site pages. Its CEO, Jeff Frost, said "Rather than continue the charade of promoting a business model that just doesn't work, we closed up shop and made a resounding cybersplat." In the very near future, I predict class action and private lawsuits brought against some of the biggest promoters of Internet malls by their tenants and site buyers based on the dramatic difference between the claims and promises made compared with the reality.

Bottom-line is: there is no rush. Take your time. Watch, study, learn, investigate, ask lots of questions, and be patient.

IS THERE A FREE LUNCH ON THE INTERNET?

If there is an eternal no B.S. truth about life, it is that "there ain't no free lunch." Ever. But that sure doesn't stop us from looking for it, does it? To quote Texas Bix Bender again: "You can always find free cheese in a mousetrap." Yep.

That brings us to the free advertising claim of the Internet. Your Web site might be seen by thousands or tens of thousands or even millions of people at almost no cost to you. Or you can use e-mail to send out thousands of sales messages with no printing or postage costs. Free marketing!

This is obviously attractive. But, the odds of people just stumbling across your Web site and becoming your customers are about the same as the odds of winning the lottery or being struck twice by lightning. You have to do things to bring prospective customers to your Web site, and all of those things either cost money or are incredibly labor intensive which means they cost time and, therefore, money.

If you decide to use the free direct mail offered by e-mail, you'd better watch out. Since its birth as a research tool, the Internet has been an adamantly anti-commercial environment and it is common for someone who sends out mass quantities of unsolicited e-mail to be spammed. This entails having huge quantities of useless e-mail sent to his or her address, often freezing the site, the server, and getting his or her service cut-off. Therefore, using e-mail for marketing purposes is possible, but very tricky, generally requiring much greater expertise than the novice or casual Internet user possesses.

IN SPITE OF ALL THAT, MAYBE YOU SHOULD BE ON THE INTERNET?

To be fair, let me quickly give you some good news: Internet users and shoppers tend, demographically, to be high income, above average education, relatively sophisticated people with diverse interests. For many businesses, these are very desirable customers.

If you're interested in global commerce, the Internet attracts a lot of people from every imaginable country. Through my Web site, we've received inquiries from or sold to people in Greece, Russia, Germany, France, England, Australia, New Zealand, Japan, Korea, and Taiwan.

Internet browsers tend to spend a lot of time at Web sites that interest them. For example, the Sharper Image catalogue people report that the average time spent at their Web site by a browser is more than ten minutes. Warner Brothers Studio Stores reports an average of 32 minutes. Visitors to my Web site are spending 10 to 20 minutes. Facts like these are encouraging and stimulating to anybody with a marketing-oriented mind.

Companies everywhere are spending a whole lot of money trying to figure out how they can turn the Internet into a truly viable marketplace and marketing medium. Maybe they will.

For now, there are other, more valuable uses of the Internet that entrepreneurs should take much more seriously. The Internet is a very efficient and powerful research tool. There are over 200 different Internet sites offering help to inventors and entrepreneurs with idea protection, copyright, trademark, patent, financing, business plan development, and licensing. The Internet is also a very useful publicity tool, because the media is using it to search out story ideas and conduct research. If you list a Web site address on news releases or correspondence with the media, chances are very good they will access it.

Possibly the best uses of the Internet have to do with communication and providing services to your existing customers or clients. If you train your customers to access your Web site, you can use it to deliver product use directions, troubleshooting answers, event schedules, new products, and all sorts of other information. Sending out customer newsletters by e-mail is a fantastic money and time saver. Mass e-mail to customers or prospects who have indicated interest is effective, easy, and virtually free.

I'm not at all opposed to the Internet. Is it just a fad, like CB Radios, that will go away? Possibly, but I don't think so. I think it's likely to be an increasingly important part of the communications process so you probably should get involved. But by all means, do it at your own pace, on your own terms.

I'm often asked for recommendations of legitimate, helpful experts. Here is the person that I recommend. His name is Ken McCarthy and he manages my own Web site. He is one of the most respected, qualified experts in this field. In fact, his book about marketing through the Internet was the first such book to be published and is widely accepted in Japan. His clients include some of the world's biggest corporations, but he also publishes how-to materials, offers seminars, and provides Web site development services for small business people. You can reach Ken at: e-media.com on the Internet. Be sure to mention that I suggested you contact him.

IF YOU WANT TO CHECK OUT WEB SITES...

Here's a list of some of the most interesting business-related and direct-selling Web sites. These have been selected from the Internet Marketing and Technology Report's 1997 review of the 100 best sites, the First American Group Purchasing Association's list of the ten best sites, and several other sources.

- www.amazon.com

- www.bacardi.com

- www.choicemall.com

- www.computereconomics.com

- www.crayola.com

- www.cy.com

- www.e-offers.com

- www.hotcoupons.com

- www.inner-circle.com

- www.lookupusa.com

- www.retailing.com

- www.score.org

- www.virtualvin.com

There are also two books I'd like to recommend, if you're interested in further exploring business on the Internet: *The World Wide Web Yellow Pages*, which lists and describes hundreds of Web sites, organized by category, just like the regular Yellow Pages telephone directories we're all used to, and *CyberBucks* by Kim Kommando. Self-Counsel Press also publishes *Doing Big Business On The Internet*, an excellent guide to business opportunities using the Internet.

THE FAX AS A MARKETING MACHINE

As reluctant as I am to express much enthusiasm for the Internet, I am in love with the fax machine. It's my opinion that the fax machine is the greatest marketing invention made during my lifetime. Here's why. It's a marketing truth that it is easier and more profitable to sell more to existing customers than to get new customers, and fax communication is an excellent way to communicate with customers frequently at a dirt-cheap cost. Customers are usually willing to provide their fax numbers and eager to get timely information from you via fax.

Taking in-bound orders by fax is very exciting. It provides the impulse-buy opportunity without (or in addition to) a manned 800-number. In businesses like mine, an order received by fax is much better than the same order called in over the phone for several reasons, including cost of taking the order and accuracy of the information.

Even very small businesses can benefit. For example, it's an increasing trend in restaurants for take-out orders to come in by fax and be ready at a separate pick-up window.

When prospecting for new business by direct mail, including a simple form that prospective customers can fax back to request more information almost always boosts responses. The ease and immediacy of faxing back a form beats the delayed reaction time involved in mailing it.

Fax-on-demand technology is proving very effective for a number of businesses. If you're not familiar with it, here's how it works: let's say you own a pet store. You can set up your fax to dispense a variety of information relevant to your business. Your menu of available materials might look like this:

- 001 Seven secrets of nutrition for healthy pets

- 002 What you need to know before buying a dog

- 003 What you need to know before buying a cat

- 004 What you need to know before buying a bird

- 005 How to save 10% to 20% on all your pet supplies

- 006 How to teach your pet to do tricks

People can call up, punch in their fax number, punch in the code, and instantly get that literature via their fax machine, even at 2 a.m., while you're sleeping and your store is closed. You are able to send out sales literature with no printing bill, no envelope stuffing, no addressing, no postage, and no delays.

Today, fax-on-demand is more prevalent in business-to-business marketing than consumer marketing, and its popularity is definitely spreading and its uses diversifying. Thanks to the explosion of home-based business activity, an ever-increasing number of homes have fax machines, and, of course, every office has one.

Broadcast fax is another excellent use of fax technology. There are all sorts of service companies who can take your list of fax numbers or use a commercially available, rented list and instantly send your fax to 100, 1,000, 10,000, or 100,000 people. Zap. Associations use this technique to market to their members, companies use it for their customers, newsletter publishers use it for their subscribers, and so on. I caution against using broadcast fax with cold leads where no permission has been given or interest expressed, but in situations where you are reasonably certain your fax will be of interest to the recipients, this is a very fast, very efficient, very cheap marketing option.

Right now, broadcast fax beats e-mail because of your ability to totally control the appearance of the sales letter or flyer being delivered. With e-mail, you are very, very limited in your ability to use different typestyles and sizes, bold facing, underlining, italicizing, etc. to enhance your message.

But when you fax, you can send the same document you would have printed and mailed.

Here are a few ways I've seen businesses effectively using faxes:

- A restaurant faxes its weekly menu of specials, daily soup-and-sandwich combos, etc. with coupons to its list of regular customers directly to their office. They report an average coupon redemption of nearly 50%!

- A seminar company faxes its sales letters for upcoming events to its VIP list of past attendees, offering early bird discounts, before it starts its regular advertising in the area.

- A vendor of used and re-built parts in the electronics industry faxes a list of Just In And Now Available parts to its customers twice a month. (This same vendor has current, frequently updated inventory and price lists of parts and products by category available via a fax-on-demand system as well as on its Web site.)

- An insurance agent faxes his tax tips newsletter to his clients every month. This saves him about $5,000 a year in postage alone.

By the way, if you want to communicate with me, you can fax me at: (602) 269-3113. I like to hear from customers and clients by fax and encourage orders to be placed by fax. This allows us to run a collection of businesses very efficiently with the absolute minimum of staff.

I love the fax machine.

VOICE MAIL AS A MARKETING TOOL: THE MAGIC OF THE FREE RECORDED MESSAGE

In and of itself, the free recorded message is not a panacea, and should be used in concert with other smart techniques. But it is clear that offering additional information or free literature to prospective customers via a free recorded message compared with having to call a regular business number and talk with a live salesperson almost always boosts responses. At the same time, the recorded message lets you, the marketer, run ads, send out mailings, and handle all the initial response without any significant staff requirements, and without your having to take calls personally.

Today, voice mail options for marketing purposes range from the simple to the incredibly sophisticated and complex. Voice mail can be linked to regular or toll-free numbers, of any length, recorded using your voice or other voice(s) of your choice, with or without background music. It can capture leads by: asking the caller to record his or her name, address, etc.; letting the caller choose options from a menu to hear his or her choice of messages; giving the caller the option of pushing a button on his or her phone to be transferred from the recording to a real person; or it can be linked to fax-on-demand.

There's even a Find Me option. Let's say you run a carpet cleaning business. A person calls to hear your free recorded message about "10 things you need to know before hiring any carpet cleaner." At the end, your customer can leave his or her name and address to have your brochure and coupons sent by mail. But what if the customer is impressed, ready to hire you, and wants to talk to somebody immediately? No problem. You give the customer that choice, he or she hits the star key on his or her phone, and — zap — your customer is transferred to your regular office phone. But what if you're a one-person operator? No problem. When your customer hits that button, he or she is transferred to your cell phone. If you don't answer after four rings, he or she is transferred to your home phone, then your office phone. At the same time, this system can notify you of the call via your beeper.

In other words, you can figure out a number of response handling options that are right for your business and tie them into your voice mail.

A COMPLEX MATRIX OF COMMUNICATION AND MARKETING TECHNOLOGIES

This is kind of incredible, but you can tie together a package of sophisticated voice mail, lead capture, fax-on-demand, e-mail receiving and sending (without being on-line), the Find Me option, and more through one phone number and one service. One of the leaders in this field is Glen Davidson at ATG Technologies, and you can contact him by fax at 1-800-800-6126. He'll be glad to send you a complete information package free of charge. Again, be sure to mention that I suggested you call.

An example of a clever way to use technology in marketing is Glen's invention, The Talking Business Sticker. A business gets a custom-printed sticker to put on the back of business cards or on a sales letter or wherever. The card entitles the recipient to ten minutes of free long-distance calls. When the individual dials up the 800 number to make the free long-distance calls, he or she first hears a promotional message for the business. The message can be updated as frequently as necessary, even daily. Isn't that incredible?

THE AMAZING POWER OF AUDIO AND VIDEO BROCHURES

Admittedly this is not new technology. But the costs keep coming down, and the value keeps going up.

I have developed talking brochures and talking sales letters for many different kinds of businesses and products, including multi-level network marketing, financial services and insurance, chiropractic care, business opportunities, and industrial equipment.

I like the talking brochure because it discourages skimming and lets you deliver a complete sales message, can offer multiple voices, sound effects, and music to make it more interesting, can include your customers' testimonials in their own voices, and can hold the attention of the listener longer than you'd be able to with printed material. I have seen the addition of this type of cassette to a direct-mail package double the number of responses.

Video brochures, often done in infomercial formats, can be extremely effective, especially in instances where product demonstrations can be made. Remember that 85% of all homes and nearly 50% of all offices have at least one VCR.

In 1996, Nintendo mailed two million video brochures to targeted prospects and made their new game the fastest selling product in the 20-year history of the video game industry. Other users of direct-mail video brochures include Toyota (for their customers), DuPont Agricultural Products (for farmers), World Wildlife Fund (for donors), and Select Comfort Mattresses (also for customers). Many of my clients use video brochures for a wide variety of purposes.

FINAL THOUGHTS ON TECHNOLOGY

I am just as opposed to technology for technology's sake as I am to creativity for creativity's sake. These things have to be held to the strict standards of practicality and profit.

It's very easy to be seduced by the hot, new technology that everybody is talking about, but it's important to keep things in perspective. Incorporate new technology into your entrepreneurial life and your business cautiously, always bearing in mind that it must measurably earn its keep.

Afterword

I hope you got some worthwhile ideas out of this book and that you enjoyed reading it as much as I enjoyed putting my thoughts and experiences onto these pages.

If you would like a free catalogue of my other books, cassettes, newsletters, schedule of my seminars, etc., or just want to write to me for any reason, I'd enjoy hearing from you. You can contact me at: 5818 N. 7th Street #103, Phoenix, Arizona 85014 or by fax at: (602) 269-3113.

Free Audio Cassette Offer

If you would like a free copy of the audio cassette "Breakthrough Success Strategies for Every Entrepreneur" by Dan Kennedy, write or fax your request to:

Dan Kennedy
5818 N. 7th Street #103
Phoenix, Arizona 85014
Fax: (602) 269-3113